quick & easy
asian desserts

delicious recipes your family will love

A delightful selection of delicious Asian desserts—including favorites like Egg Tarts, Pineapple Tarts, Mango Pudding and Red Rubies in Sweet Coconut Cream.

T0166306

TUTTLE PUBLISHING
Tokyo • Rutland, Vermont • Singapore

Contents

MAIL ORDER SOURCES

Finding the ingredients for Asian home cooking has become very simple. Most super-markets carry staples such as soy sauce, fresh ginger, and fresh lemongrass. Almost every large metropolitan area has Asian markets serving the local population—just check your local business directory. With the Internet, exotic Asian ingredients and cooking utensils can be easily found online. The following list is a good starting point of online merchants offering a wide variety of goods and services.

http://www.asiafoods.com

http://www.geocities.com/MadisonAvenue/8074/VarorE.html

http://dmoz.org/Shopping/Food/Ethnic_and_Regional/Asian/

http://templeofthai.com/

http://www.orientalpantry.com/

http://www.zestyfoods.com/

http://www.thaigrocer.com/Merchant/index.htm

http://asianwok.com/

http://pilipinomart.com/

http://www.indiangrocerynet.com/

http://www.orientalfoodexpress.com/

No one can resist a delicious cake or pudding or sweet dish, especially in Asia! As in other parts of the world, this usually generates the greatest enthusiasm at family gatherings and on festive occasions. Asian desserts have yet to be popularized outside of Asia simply because they are rarely served in restaurants. Many non-Asians therefore assume that "Asian's don't often eat dessert." Nothing could be further from the truth!

Asian desserts are often served as snacks in between meals rather than after a heavy meal (when no one has room for desserts anyway). How sensible! Ask anyone with a sweet tooth and they'll tell you there's an Asian dessert for every occasion. Luscious desserts such as Indonesian Banana Custard Surprise are great for parties, while chilled desserts such as Malaysia's Sago and Honeydew Melon in Coconut Milk are perfect after meals. Filipino Egg and Milk Bonbons or Tropical Lime Pie are ideal afternoon snacks. Some rice-based desserts—Fluffy Sweet Rice Cakes springs to mind—can even become substantial meals in their own right (although perhaps to the detriment of your waistline).

It is not surprising that rice flour features prominently in many Asian dessert recipes—rice is, after all, the basic staple in most of Asia and can be found in almost every Asian pantry. And if you haven't tried rice flour desserts before, you are in for a real treat! The flavor and texture is very different from that of normal boiled rice. It is prepared in many ways—steamed, baked, boiled and fried—and tastes different each time. Exotic rice varieties such as glutinous rice as well as other grains and starches like barley, tapioca, yam and sago provide added variety. Many other delightful dessert ingredients such as coconut cream, palm sugar, bananas, mangoes, water chestnuts, cashew nuts, honeydew melon and pandanus leaves each add their own dimension to the mix.

Many people think that Asian desserts are difficult to prepare but actually most recipes are quite simple. The trick is to find the right ingredients, understand how they are used, and then master a few simple techniques. Banana leaves, for example, are often used to wrap puddings and sweets before steaming or boiling. You can buy them fresh or frozen in most parts of the world now in speciality shops, but just remember to lightly "toast" them over a flame or steam them for a few seconds before using or you won't be able to bend them. And if you can't find them, aluminum foil makes a good substitute (though it lacks the delicate fragrance of banana leaves!).

So don't be put off just because you see a few things in the recipes you are not familiar with. Almost everything is available and each new item opens up a whole new world of possibilities.

Essential Ingredients

Banana leaves are used to wrap food prior to steaming or grilling. The moisture within the banana leaf makes a difference to the texture and flavor of the food, but if you can't find fresh or frozen banana leaves, use aluminum foil. Before using them to wrap food, the leaves should be softened for easy folding, either by soaking them in hot water for 5–10 minutes or briefly heating them over a low flame.

Coconut cream and **coconut milk** are used in many Asian desserts much the same way that cow's milk and cream are used in the West. To obtain fresh **coconut cream**, grate the flesh of 1 coconut into a bowl (this yields about 3 cups of **grated fresh coconut**), add ¹/₂ cup (125 ml) water and knead a few times, then squeeze the mixture firmly with your hand or strain using a muslin cloth or cheese cloth. **Thick coconut milk** is obtained by the same method but by adding more water to the grated flesh (about 1 cup/250 ml instead of ¹/₂ cup/125 ml). **Thin coconut milk** is obtained by pressing the coconut a second time—adding 1 cup (250 ml) of water to the same grated coconut and squeezing it again. Although freshly pressed milk has more flavor, coconut cream and milk are now widely sold canned or in packets that are quick, convenient and quite tasty. Canned or packet coconut cream or milk comes in varying consistencies depending on the brand, and you will need to try them out and adjust the thickness by adding water as needed. In general, you should add 1 cup (250 ml) of water to 1 cup (250 ml) of canned or packet coconut cream to obtain thick coconut milk, and 2 cups (500 ml) of water to 1 cup (250 ml) of coconut cream to obtain thin coconut milk. These mixing ratios are only general guides however.

Calamansi limes are much smaller than regular limes. They add an aromatic citrus flavor to desserts and are available fresh in most Asian grocery stores. If calamansi limes are not available, use regular limes.

Cardamom pods are used to flavor many Indian sweets. Split them open and you will find tiny black **cardamom seeds** inside the pods which are also sold both whole and ground. If possible, buy whole pods. They are available in Asian food markets and well-stocked supermarkets.

Cream of tartar (potassium hydrogen tartrate) is a component of baking powder. It is sometimes added to candies or frostings to give them a creamier texture because it can help to prevent the crystallization of cooked sugar. Cream of tartar is also used to stabilize egg whites when making meringue. Available at the baking section in most well-stocked supermarkets.

Dried mung beans are small yellow beans with a bright green seed coat. An important ingredient in Asian desserts, mung beans should be soaked in cold water for several hours and then boiled until tender.

Dried sago pearls or **tapioca pearls** are tiny beads made from sago or cassava starch. The uncooked pearls are hard and white when dry, but turn soft and translucent when cooked. The pearls are sold in plastic packets in Asian markets.

Semolina flour is coarsely ground durum wheat, similar to couscous. Available at most well-stocked supermarkets and gourmet grocers.

Gelatin is a tasteless and colorless thickening agent that forms a jelly when dissolved in hot water and then cooled. Unlike agar-agar (another thickening agent made from seaweed), it is made from boiled animal bones and tendons. Used in jellied desserts, gelatin is sold in small packets of fine, white powder, although it is also sold in sheets or granules. Purchase unflavored gelatin for the recipes in this book.

Gingko nuts are oval and cream-colored, with hard shells that must be cracked open with a nutcracker. The inner meats have a nutty, slightly bitter flavor and must be soaked in boiling water to loosen their skins. There is a germ within the gingko nut which needs to be removed as it is quite bitter. This can be done by either splitting the nut into half and removing it, or by gently digging it out using a toothpick. Shelled nuts may be purchased frozen or refrigerated in vacuum-sealed packs in health food stores. Canned gingko nuts are also available but have less flavor—add them in the final stages of cooking.

Glutinous rice is a type of short-grained sticky rice that is widely used in Asia, often in desserts. Buy glutinous rice in the packaged grains section of supermarkets. Look for intact kernels that aren't broken, scratched or damaged. Store in a cool, dry area in a sealed glass or plastic container, away from open air and moisture. Glutinous rice comes in white or black varieties.

Glutinous rice flour is ground from white glutinous rice grains. It is stickier than normal rice flour and is generally used in sweet buns and pastries. Glutinous rice flour made from black sweet rice is black or dark purple.

Green pea flour, or **mung bean flour** is a fine, white starch obtained from mung beans. It is used to make jellies (see the recipe on page 84) and cellophane noodles. Cornstarch or arrowroot starch may be substituted.

Nutmegs are the seeds of the nutmeg tree. They are covered by a lacy red web known as mace, which is also used as a spice. Dried nutmegs should be grated or crushed just before using.

Palm sugar is the sweet sap harvested from sugar or coconut palm trees. Palm sugar varies greatly in color, consistencies and sweetness—from the soft, gooey and creamy beige type which is sold

in plastic jars to the hard and dark crystallized palm sugar sold in round disks or blocks. The dark brown palm sugar is generally sweeter and more fragrant than the others, although all types can be used for most recipes. If you cannot find palm sugar, use dark brown sugar or maple syrup. Hard palm sugar should be shaved or grated into small chunks or melted in the microwave before using. Store palm sugar in the same way as normal sugar.

Pandanus leaves are long and slender green leaves of a member of the pandanus palm or screwpine family. They impart a sweet floral fragrance to popular Southeast Asian desserts. Their intense green color is also used as a natural food coloring. Pound or process a bunch of pandanus leaves in a blender with a little water, then strain through a fine sieve to obtain **pandanus extract** (see recipe on page 8). Bottled pandanus extract is also

available. Asians use pandanus in the same way Westerners use vanilla in their cooking. Rose or vanilla extract can be used as a substitute for sweet dishes.

Pearl barley is obtained by removing the outer husks from barley grains. The grains are boiled until tender for use in Asian desserts, and are sold in most Asian grocery stores.

Rice flour is made from uncooked rice grains that are ground to a powder. To make 1 cup of rice flour, soak $^3/_4$ cup (150 g) uncooked rice in water for 5 hours, then drain and grind it slowly in a blender. Packets of rice flour are readily available in supermarkets and grocers.

Sweetened condensed milk is sold in cans in supermarkets and grocery stores. If unavailable, you can make your own. Combine 2 cups (500 ml) of fresh milk and $1^1/_4$ cups (225 g) of sugar in a large saucepan. Simmer over low heat, stirring frequently to prevent scorching, until the mixture thickens, about 45 minutes. Remove from the heat immediately and set aside to cool. The mixture will thicken further as it cools. Store in a covered container in the refrigerator. This makes about 1¼ (300 ml) cups of sweetened condensed milk.

Tapioca flour is obtained from the strained pulp of cassava roots that have been dried to a paste and then ground. The paste is heated to form small beads known as tapioca pearls. Both tapioca starch and tapioca pearls are used as thickeners, and tapioca pearls are also eaten whole in desserts.

Water chestnuts have thin brown skins and crispy, sweet flesh that retains its crunchy texture when cooked. They are available fresh from Asian grocery stores or canned from supermarkets.

Young coconut is sold canned or frozen (known as *buko* in the Philippines). Young coconuts have a gelatinous center, with a texture similar to a soft, ripe melon. The flesh has a fresh, fruity almost nutty flavor, not overly sweet. It is available fresh at fruit stalls in Asian markets. Canned young coconut is also available at supermarkets. To cut open a fresh young coconut, swiftly chop off a small part of the coconut shell with a cleaver or a heavy knife. Collect the **coconut juice** in a bowl. Cut the coconut in half and then scrape out the tender white **young coconut meat** with a spoon.

Basic Recipes

Palm Sugar Syrup

Palm Sugar Syrup is used as a sweetener in numerous Asian desserts.

⅔ cup (150 ml) water
1¼ cups (250 g) shaved palm sugar or dark brown sugar

Makes ¾ cup (190 ml)
Preparation time: 5 mins
Cooking time: 10 mins

1 Place the water and palm sugar in a saucepan. Bring to a boil and simmer over medium heat until the sugar completely dissolves and the mixture becomes syrupy.
2 Remove from the heat, set aside to cool then strain into a jar or bowl.

Sweet Coconut Pancake Filling

This savory filling is used to make Sweet Coconut Filled Pancakes (see recipe on page 53).

$3/4$ cup (135 g) shaved palm sugar or dark brown sugar
$1/4$ cup (60 ml) water
1 pandanus leaf, knotted
1 cup (100 g) grated fresh coconut or $1/2$ cup (75 g) dried coconut flakes

Makes 1 cup (250 g)
Preparation time: **20 mins**
Cooking time: **10 mins**

1 Place the palm sugar and water in a pan and cook until the sugar completely dissolves. Simmer for 10 minutes until the liquid starts to thicken and become syrupy.
2 Add the pandanus leaf and grated coconut (if using dried coconut flakes, you will need to add more water) and continue cooking over low heat for 10–15 minutes until the coconut filling is thick and glossy. Most of the liquid should have evaporated. Cool and use as desired.

Pandanus Extract

This pandanus extract adds a unique fragrance to Coconut Filled Pancakes on page 53. Choose mature, dark green pandanus leaves for maximum flavor and color.

8–10 fresh pandanus leaves
1 cup (250 ml) water

Makes $3/4$ cup (190 ml)
Preparation time: **20 mins**
Cooking time: **10 mins**

1 Rinse the pandanus leaves and, using kitchen scissors or a sharp knife, cut the leaves into short lengths.
2 Place the leaves and water in a blender and process until pulverized. Pour through a fine strainer and discard the solids. Measure out the required amount of juice as specified in the recipe.

Creamy Egg Tarts

4 large eggs
1 cup (200 g) sugar
$^1/_2$ teaspoon salt
$2^1/_2$ cups (625 ml) milk
1 teaspoon vanilla extract

Pie Crust
$1^1/_4$ cups (185 g) flour,
  plus extra for dusting
$^1/_4$ teaspoon salt
$^1/_4$ cup ($^1/_2$ stick/60 g)
  chilled butter, diced
2 tablespoons chilled
  vegetable shortening,
  finely diced
3–4 tablespoons iced
  water
Lightly floured greaseproof
  paper, for wrapping

1 Make the Pie Crust by sifting the flour and salt into a large bowl. Add the diced butter and shortening and mix with the flour until the mixture resembles coarse breadcrumbs. Slowly add in the iced water, knead the dough until it forms a ball. Wrap in the floured grease-proof paper and chill in the refrigerator for 30 minutes.
2 Divide the dough into 8 portions. Roll out each portion until it is $^1/_8$ in (3 mm) thick and forms a circle. Press the dough onto the sides and bottoms of the custard cups. Make sure no air is trapped between the dough and each cup. Preheat the oven to 425°F (220°C).
3 Beat the eggs with the other ingredients in a large mixing bowl. Strain and pour into each Pie Crust. Bake for 30 minutes, or until a knife inserted into the center of each tart comes out clean.

Serves 8
Preparation time: **15 mins + 30 mins for chilling pie crust**
Cooking time: **30 mins**

Tropical Lime Pie

The humble calamansi lime adds a tang to this rich, creamy pie while the crust made from graham crackers or finger biscuits is wonderfully innovative.

Pie Crust
$3/4$ cup (75 g) graham cracker or finger biscuit crumbs
3 tablespoons sugar
$1/4$ cup ($1/2$ stick/60 g) melted butter

Filling
$1/4$ cup (60 ml) water
1 tablespoon unflavored gelatin powder
2 cups (500 ml) whipping cream, well chilled
$1 1/4$ cups (300 ml) sweetened condensed milk
$1/4$ cup (60 ml) fresh calamansi lime juice or freshly-squeezed regular lime juice
Whipped cream for topping (optional)

Serves 8
Preparation time: **40 mins + 6 hours for chilling**
Cooking time: **10 mins**

1 Preheat the oven to 350°F (180°C).
2 To make the Pie Crust, mix the graham cracker or finger biscuit crumbs, sugar and melted butter. Press the mixture into a 9-in (23-cm) pie plate and chill for about 15 minutes. Bake the crust for about 5 minutes in the preheated oven. Set aside to cool.
3 To make the Filling, pour the water into a small saucepan and sprinkle the unflavored gelatin powder on top. Set aside for 5 minutes to allow the gelatin to swell. Heat over low heat, stirring until the liquid clears and the gelatin completely dissolves, about 3 minutes. Set aside.
4 Beat the whipping cream with a mixer at medium speed for 5 minutes. Slowly add the condensed milk and lime juice and beat to blend, about 2 minutes. Add the gelatin mixture and beat until the mixture is smooth. Chill for 5–10 minutes, or until partially set.
5 Spoon the Filling into the cooled Pie Crust. Chill for 6 hours before serving, topped with whipped cream, if desired.

Calamansi limes are smaller than regular limes, and their juice is used in marinades and dips. They add an aromatic citrus flavor to desserts and are available fresh in most Asian grocery stores. If calamansi limes are not available, substitute regular limes.

Finger biscuits are sweet, crumbly biscuits sold in packets in supermarkets. If finger biscuits are not available, substitute any other sweet, crumbly biscuits.

Banana Cream Pie

2 ripe bananas (approx 8 oz/250 g), peeled and sliced, sprinkled with lemon juice to prevent discoloration
Greaseproof paper, dusted with flour
Flour, for dusting

Pie Crust

1¹/₄ cups (185 g) flour, plus extra for dusting
¹/₄ teaspoon salt
¹/₄ cup (¹/₂ stick/60 g) chilled butter, diced
2 tablespoons chilled vegetable shortening, diced
3–4 tablespoons iced water

Filling

2 cups (500 ml) cream or evaporated milk
6 tablespoons flour
¹/₄ cup (50 g) sugar
4 eggs
1 tablespoon butter
1 teaspoon vanilla extract
Whipped cream, to serve (optional)

Serves 6–8
Preparation time: **20 mins + 45 mins for chilling Pie Crust**
Cooking time: **35–45 mins**

1 Preheat the oven to 390°F (200°C).

2 To make the Pie Crust, sift the flour and salt into a large bowl. Mix the diced butter and shortening into the flour until the mixture resembles coarse breadcrumbs.

3 Gradually add in the iced water to the mixture, knead the dough until it forms a ball. Sprinkle some flour on a greaseproof paper and wrap the dough with the paper. Chill in the refrigerator for 30 minutes.

4 Sprinkle some flour on a clean work surface. Using a floured rolling pin, roll out the chilled dough, starting from the center and lifting the rolling pin just before it reaches the edge. Roll the dough until it is ¹/₈ in (3 mm) thick and forms a circle, 2–3 in (5–7.5 cm) larger than a 9-in (23-cm) pie plate.

5 Lift the dough and ease it onto the pie plate. Press the dough firmly onto the bottom and sides of the plate. Make sure no air is trapped between the dough and the plate. Do not stretch the dough, or it will shrink.

6 Using kitchen scissors, trim any excess dough from the edge of the pie plate, leaving a 1¹/₂-in (4-cm) overhang. Fold the dough under the edge of the plate and flute or decorate edge as desired. Put the dough in the freezer for 15 minutes.

7 Use a fork to pierce small holes in the surface and sides of the Pie Crust to allow steam to escape during baking. Line the crust with baking paper and fill with pie weights or dry beans. and bake in the preheated oven for 10–12 minutes. Transfer to a rack, remove the baking paper and pie weights or dry beans. Bake for 5 more minutes, or until golden brown.

8 To make the Filling, heat the cream or evaporated milk in a saucepan. Mix the flour, sugar and eggs in a bowl until smooth. Whip in the heated cream or milk. Return to the saucepan and simmer, stirring to form a smooth mixture, about 20 minutes.

9 Blend in the butter and vanilla extract. Spoon half of the Filling into the baked pie crust. Add the banana rounds. Top with the remaining Filling and whipped cream, if desired.

Mango Pie with Roasted Cashews

1 cup (250 ml) coconut cream or thick coconut milk

$^1/_2$ cup (100 g) sugar

$^1/_2$ cup (125 ml) sweetened condensed milk

$^1/_3$ cup (85 g) custard powder

1 cup (250 g) canned pumpkin purée or pie filling

$^1/_2$ cup (75 g) chopped roasted cashew nuts

2 eggs

2 tablespoons rum

$^1/_2$ teaspoon ground cinnamon

1 teaspoon finely grated fresh ginger

1 piece pastry dough to fit a pie pan, (9 in/ 23 cm) in diameter

Toppings

2 ripe mangoes

$^1/_2$ cup (125 ml) bottled mango or apricot jam (purchased)

Whipped cream or ice cream, to serve

1 Preheat the oven to 425°F (220°C).

2 Make the pie filling by combining the coconut cream, sugar, condensed milk and custard powder in a mixing bowl. Stir until the sugar completely dissolves. Add the pumpkin and chopped nuts. Beat in the eggs lightly and then add the rum, cinnamon and ginger.

3 Pour the mixture into the pastry dough. Bake for 15 minutes at 425°F (220°C), then reduce the heat to 300°F (150°C) and bake until set, about 15–20 minutes. Remove from the oven, set aside to cool and place in the refrigerator to chill.

4 Prepare the Toppings by peeling and cutting each mango into two halves around the seed. Slice each half into very thin slices.

5 Melt the jam in a small saucepan over low heat.

6 Arrange the sliced mangoes on top of the cold pie and brush the surface with a first coat of the jam. Return to the refrigerator to cool and then repeat the process to give two more coats for a nice and shiny seal.

7 To serve, slice the pie and top each piece with whipped cream or ice cream.

Serves 4–6
Preparation time: 30 mins
Cooking time: 50 mins

Cashew Tarts

Crust

1 1/2 cups (250 g) flour
2 1/2 tablespoons sugar
1/4 teaspoon baking soda
1/4 teaspoon salt
1/2 cup (1 stick/125 g) butter
1 egg yolk, lightly beaten
1 tablespoon lemon juice
6 tablespoons iced water
Greaseproof paper, dusted with flour
Flour, for dusting

Cashew Filling

3 eggs
1 cup (200 g) sugar
1 cup (250 ml) maple syrup or pancake syrup
2 tablespoons melted butter, plus extra for greasing the molds
1 teaspoon vanilla extract
1 cup (150 g) finely chopped cashew nuts

1 Preheat the oven to 350°F (180°C).

2 To make the Crust, sift together the flour, sugar, baking soda and salt in a bowl. Dice the butter and mix with the flour until the mixture resembles coarse breadcrumbs. Add the egg yolk and lemon juice. Add the iced water, 1 tablespoon at a time, and knead until the dough can be formed into a ball. Wrap the dough in the prepared greaseproof paper and chill for 30 minutes.

3 To make the Cashew Filling, combine all the ingredients and set aside.

4 Sprinkle some flour onto a clean work surface. Using a floured rolling pin, roll out the Crust onto the floured work surface until it is 1/8 in (3 mm) thick. Using an inverted tart mold or a sharp knife, cut out the dough to fit the tart molds. Combine and roll the remaining dough and repeat the process to make 20 pieces.

5 Brush the tart molds with melted butter and place the cut pieces of dough into each mold.

6 Place about 1 tablespoon of the Cashew Filling into each mold. Bake in the preheated oven for 20–25 minutes or until the pastry is light brown and the Filling is just firm (it will continue to firm up for a few minutes after it has been removed from the oven). Remove the tarts from the molds and wrap in cellophane if desired, or store in an airtight container if not serving immediately.

Makes about 20 tarts
Preparation time: 30 mins + 30 mins chilling time
Cooking time: 20–25 mins

Pineapple Tarts

1¹/₂ cups (225 g) flour
Pinch of salt
¹/₂ cup (1 stick/125 g)
  chilled butter, diced
1 egg
1 teaspoon lemon juice
2 egg whites
Whole cloves, to garnish
  (optional)

Pineapple Filling
1 small ripe pineapple,
  (about 2 lbs/1 kg),
  peeled, cored and
  chopped
³/₄ cup (185 g) soft
  brown sugar, or more
  to taste
1 tablespoon lemon
  juice
3 cloves
2 star anise pods
¹/₂ teaspoon freshly
  grated nutmeg

Makes 30 tarts
Preparation time: 10 mins
Cooking time: 25 mins

1 Make the Pineapple Filling by processing the pineapple in a food processor or blender until coarsely ground, about 10 seconds. Transfer to a non-stick saucepan with a heavy base. Add the sugar, lemon juice, cloves, star anise and nutmeg. Simmer uncovered over medium-high heat, stirring frequently with a wooden spoon, until thick, about 20–25 minutes. Transfer to a shallow bowl and set aside to cool. Remove the cloves and star anise pods.

2 Mix the flour, salt and butter together until the mixture resembles coarse breadcrumbs. Add the egg and lemon juice and knead until it forms a ball. Put in a plastic bag and refrigerate for 30 minutes. Preheat the oven to 350°F (180°C)

3 Roll out the dough very thinly on a floured board. Use a cutter to cut out 30 circles, each 2¹/₂ in (6 cm) in diameter. Press into well-greased tartlet or cupcake molds, fluting the edges with a pastry cutter or a fork. Fill each pastry with 1 teaspoon of the Pineapple Filling. Brush with egg white and top with a clove, if desired.

4 Bake at 350°F (180°C) until golden brown, about 20 minutes. Remove from the oven, loosen the tarts with a knife and transfer to racks to cool. Store in an airtight container when completely cooled.

This recipe results in light, firm and flakey tarts. Another alternative to fluting the edges of the pastry is to cut the dough with a cookie cutter that has scalloped or serrated edges. Then, push each piece of dough into a cupcake tray to shape it.

Mango Coconut Tart

Dough

2 cups (300 g) all purpose flour

$^1/_2$ cup (100 g) sugar

6 tablespoons butter or shortening

1 egg

4 tablespoons coconut milk, adding more as needed

1 teaspoon vanilla extract

Filling

2 cups (500 ml) coconut cream or thick coconut milk

$^1/_2$ cup (100 g) sugar

4 eggs, beaten

1 teaspoon vanilla extract

$^1/_4$ cup (25 g) sweetened coconut flakes

Toppings

2 ripe mangoes

$^1/_2$ cup (125 ml) bottled mango or apricot jam (purchased)

Whipped cream or ice cream, to serve

Serves 4–6

Preparation time: 30 mins

Cooking time: 30 mins

1 Combine all the Dough ingredients in a mixing bowl, mix well and knead until smooth. Alternatively, you may purchase ready-made pie dough if you do not wish to make your own. Roll the Dough out into a flat sheet, less than $^1/_8$ in (3 mm) thick. Cut the Dough to fit into 10 small well-greased tartlet pans or one large 10-in (25-cm) pie plate.

2 Preheat the oven to 360°F (180°C).

3 To make the Filling, combine the coconut cream and sugar in a pot over medium heat and cook until the mixture just comes to a gentle boil. Do not allow the mixture to come to a full boil, but immediately remove from the heat and set aside to cool until lukewarm.

4 Slowly stir the egg and vanilla extract into the lukewarm coconut cream mixture. Strain the mixture through a fine sieve into a bowl. Gently fold in the coconut flakes.

5 Pour the coconut mixture into the tartlet shells or the pie shell until about $^3/_4$ full. Do not fill to the rim. Place the pans in the oven and bake until the custard is set—when a knife inserted into the middle of the Filling comes out clean—about 15–20 minutes. Remove the tartlets or pie from the oven and allow to cool. Refrigerate to cool further.

6 Prepare the Toppings by peeling and cutting each mango into halves, removing the pits. Slice the halves thinly and set aside. Melt the mango or apricot jam in a saucepan over low heat.

7 Arrange the thin mango slices on top of the cold tarts and brush the top with a first coat of the melted jam. Return to the refrigerator to cool and then repeat the process for a 2nd or 3rd coat to get a nice and shiny seal all over the top. Serve cold with whipped cream or ice cream.

Mango Refrigerator Cake

6 large ripe mangoes (about $6^1/_2$ lbs/3 kg)
Two and half packets (75 sticks) lady finger biscuits ($6^1/_2$ oz/200 g per packet)
2 cups (500 ml) canned mango juice
Three x 8-oz (250-g) pack cream cheese
2 cups (500 ml) heavy cream
3 cups (375 g) confectioner's (icing) sugar

Serves 4–5
Preparation time: 40 mins
Chilling time: 4–5 hours

1 Peel the mangoes and slice the flesh away from the pits, then slice the flesh thinly. Divide into three equal portions and set aside.

2 Divide the biscuits into 3 portions. Work with one portion at a time. Dip the biscuits, one at a time, into the mango juice. Arrange the biscuits in a 12 x 8 x 2 in (30 x 20 x 5 cm) baking pan, with the tops of the biscuits facing down.

3 Beat together the cream cheese and heavy cream in an electric mixer. Gradually add the sugar and continue beating until the mixture is smooth. Divide the cream cheese mixture into three equal portions.

4 Spread 1 portion of the cream cheese mixture over the biscuits. Arrange one portion of the mango wedges over the cream cheese mixture.

5 Dip the second portion of biscuits, one at a time, in the mango juice and layer over the mangoes. Spread one portion of the cream cheese mixture on the biscuits and arrange one portion of the mangoes on top.

6 Dip the remaining biscuits in the mango juice, one at a time, and arrange on top of the mangoes. Spread the remaining cream cheese mixture on the biscuits. Arrange the remaining mango wedges on top. Chill for 4–5 hours, or until firm, before serving.

Lady finger biscuits are sweet, crumbly biscuits sold in packets in supermarkets. Graham crackers may be substituted if lady finger biscuits are not available. There are 27 sheets in each box (14 oz/408 g) of graham crackers. Each sheet can be broken down into 4 pieces. One other substitute for finger biscuits will be the "broas" sold at Filipino specialty stores.

Quick Banana Cake

Softened butter, for
brushing
2 ripe bananas (approx
8 oz/250 g), peeled
2 teaspoon lime juice
$1/2$ cup (1 stick/125 g)
butter
$3/4$ cup (150 g) fine granulated sugar
3 medium eggs, beaten
Pinch of baking soda
$1^1/_4$ cups (185 g) self-
rising flour

Makes 1 cake
Preparation time: **40 mins**
Cooking time: **40–45 mins**

1 Preheat the oven to 350°F (170°C).

2 Grease the inside of a 7-in (18-cm) round or square baking pan with the softened butter.

3 In a small bowl, mash the bananas with a fork and stir in the lime juice. Set aside.

4 Cream the butter and sugar together with an electric mixer or wooden spoon until light and fluffy. Pour in the eggs, a little at a time, beating well in between additions.

5 Using a large metal spoon, fold in the baking soda and half the flour without over-stirring or beating the mixture (which would otherwise make the cake flat and heavy). Fold in the mashed bananas until well incorporated and then add the remaining flour.

6 Turn the mixture out into the prepared pan. Hollow out the middle slightly to prevent it rising to a dome in the middle. Bake in the preheated oven for about 40 minutes or until the cake is well risen and golden brown. To test if the cake is cooked, insert a knife in the center—it should come out clean.

7 Allow the cake to cool in the pan for 10 minutes before running a knife around the edges and turning it out to cool on a wire rack.

Cinnamon Layer Cake

$^1/_4$ cup ($^1/_2$ stick/60 g) butter, melted

$^1/_2$ cup (125 g) ground cinnamon

$^1/_2$ cup (125 g) freshly grated nutmeg

Vanilla ice cream, to serve (optional)

Batter

$^1/_2$ cup (100 g) fine granulated sugar

5 egg yolks

$^2/_3$ cup (100 g) flour, sifted

1$^1/_2$ cups (375 ml) thick coconut milk

Serves 4
Preparation time: 15 mins
Cooking time: About
1 hour (5 mins per layer)

1 Preheat the oven to 350°F (180°C).

2 To make the Batter, beat the sugar and egg yolks together until the sugar completely dissolves, then stir in the flour. Gradually stir in the coconut milk, mixing to combine thoroughly.

3 Dip a brush in the melted butter and paint the sides of a small, deep baking pan about 6 in (15 cm) in diameter, or a loaf pan about 7 x 3 in (18 x 7.5 cm). Pour in 2–3 ladles of the Batter to make a thin layer about $^1/_4$ in (6 mm) thick.

4 Sprinkle the top with 2 teaspoons ground cinnamon and 2 teaspoons grated nutmeg. Set the baking pan in a baking dish of hot water and bake in the preheated oven until just set, about 5 minutes. Remove the baking pan from the oven and brush the top of the cooked layer with melted butter. Pour in another 2–3 ladles of Batter to make another thin layer and sprinkle with 2 teaspoons grated nutmeg and 2 teaspoons ground cinnamon. Return to the oven and bake until set.

5 Repeat until the Batter is used up, brushing the top of each newly cooked layer with butter before adding the batter and spices.

6 When the last layer has cooked, remove from the oven and allow to cool in the pan. When cooled, loosen the edges with a knife and turn the cake upside down onto a serving plate. Serve chilled with a scoop of vanilla ice cream, if desired.

Steamed Caramel Cakes

³/₄ cup (150 g) sugar
¹/₂ cup (125 ml) hot
  water
¹/₄ cup (¹/₂ stick/60 g)
  butter, melted
¹/₄ cup (65 ml) cream or
  evaporated milk
1 egg, beaten
1¹/₄ cups (185 g) flour
1 teaspoon baking soda
Pinch of salt
¹/₄ cup (50 g) + 2 tea-
  spoons sugar

Serves 6–8
Preparation time: 30 mins
Cooking time: 30–40 mins

1 Melt ³/₄ cup (150 g) of sugar in a small heavy-based saucepan over very low heat until it caramelizes and turns golden brown. Remove the pan from the heat.
2 Pour the hot water onto the caramel—be careful not to get burned as the caramel will splutter. Boil the caramel for a few minutes until completely melted and a syrup is formed. Allow the syrup to cool and pour into a measuring cup—you need ²/₃ cup (150 ml). If you have less, add a little water to make up the specified quantity. Add the melted butter, milk and egg to the caramel syrup. Stir well to combine.
3 Sift the flour, baking soda and salt into a mixing bowl. Stir in the sugar. Make a well in the center and pour in the caramel syrup. Stir gently with a wooden spoon to make a smooth batter.
4 Fill small, lightly-buttered tartlet trays or rice wine cups three-quarters full of batter and steam until set, about 15–20 minutes, depending on size of trays or cups used.

Young Coconut Meringue Cake

6 egg yolks
$^3/_4$ cup (150 g) sugar
$^1/_2$ teaspoon vanilla extract
$^1/_3$ cup (50 g) flour
$^1/_2$ cup (125 ml) sweetened condensed milk
$^1/_2$ cup (125 ml) warm water
Flesh of 4 young coconuts

Meringue Topping
6 egg whites
1 tablespoon sugar
$^1/_4$ teaspoon salt
$^1/_2$ cup (75 g) raisins

1 Preheat the oven to 400°F (200°C).
2 Beat the egg yolks, sugar and vanilla extract until the sugar completely dissolves and the mixture becomes pale and foamy.
3 Put the flour in a saucepan and gradually stir in the condensed milk and water. Add the coconut flesh. Stir in the beaten egg yolks.
4 Cook over medium heat, stirring for 5 minutes until the mixture thickens. Transfer the mixture to a heat-proof dish.
5 Make the Meringue Topping by beating the egg whites, sugar and salt together until the mixture is stiff. Spread over the cake and scatter the raisins on top. Bake in the preheated oven until the meringue turns golden brown, about 15 minutes.

Serves: 4–6
Preparation time: **15 mins**
Cooking time: **25 mins**

Pineapple Semolina Cake with Pistachios

1 1/4 cups (250 g) fine granulated sugar
3 cups (750 ml) water
1/2 cup (125 ml) melted butter
2 cups (300 g) fine semolina flour
1 teaspoon ground cardamom
One 16-oz (450-g) can pineapple, drained and chopped
1 cup (130 g) shelled pistachio nuts, chopped
One 10-in (25-cm) square baking pan, lightly greased

1 Boil the sugar and water in a saucepan for 5 minutes to form a thick syrup. Remove from the heat and allow to cool in a warm place.

2 Heat the butter in a heavy saucepan and stir-fry the semolina and ground cardamom over low heat for 5 minutes until it becomes slightly darker. Add the syrup and stir to mix well. Cover tightly and simmer for 10–15 minutes until almost all the water has evaporated. By this time, the semolina should be soft. If the semolina grains are still uncooked, add more water, cover and cook over low heat until they are soft and cooked. Add the pineapple and pistachio nuts, and mix well.

3 Press the cooked semolina mixture into the baking pan and spread it out evenly. Allow to cool and set. Then cut into squares and serve.

Serves 6   Preparation time: **20 mins**
Cooking time: **25 mins**

Banana Coconut Cake

1 cup (125 g) rice flour
$^1/_2$ tablespoon salt
$^3/_4$ cup (150 g) shaved palm sugar or dark brown sugar
$^1/_2$ cup (125 ml) water
$^1/_2$ teaspoon ground cardamom
6 ripe bananas (about 1$^2/_3$ lbs/750 g), peeled and thinly sliced
1 cup (100 g) grated fresh coconut or $^1/_2$ cup (75 g) dried coconut flakes
4 tablespoons melted butter

Serves 6
Preparation time: **15 mins**
Cooking time: **30 mins**

1 Line a steamer with a muslin cloth, spread the rice flour on it and steam for 10 minutes. Alternatively, dry-fry the rice flour in a wok for 5–10 minutes over low heat. Set aside to cool thoroughly, then sift the flour into a mixing bowl, removing any lumps.
2 Combine the salt, sugar and water in a bowl and mix well. Drizzle the mixture on top of the flour and then mix until it resembles fine breadcrumbs. Add the ground cardamom and mix well.
3 Place $^1/_3$ of the rice flour mixture into a heat-proof casserole dish. Layer $^1/_2$ of the banana slices on top of the flour mixture and top with $^1/_2$ of the grated coconut. Add another layer of the rice flour mixture, banana and coconut, and finish with the final layer of the flour mixture. Drizzle the butter over the top evenly.
4 Steam the mixture for 30 minutes in a covered steamer until cooked. Remove from the heat, slice and serve hot.

Coconut Chestnut Cupcakes

1 cup ($^1/_2$ lb/250 g)
peeled and diced water
chestnuts
2$^1/_2$ cups (625 ml) water
$^1/_2$ cup (65 g) rice flour
1 teaspoon Pandanus
Extract (page 8)
$^3/_4$ cup (150 g) sugar

Topping
$^1/_3$ cup (40 g) rice flour
1$^1/_2$ cups (375 ml) thick
coconut milk
4 tablespoons sugar
$^3/_4$ teaspoon salt

Serves 8
Preparation time: 30 mins
Cooking time: 30 mins

1 Boil the diced water chestnut with 1$^1/_2$ cups (375 ml) of the water in a saucepan over medium heat until soft, about 5 minutes. Remove and drain. Set aside.
2 Combine the rice flour, 1 cup (250 ml) water and Pandanus Extract in a saucepan and mix well. Simmer over medium heat for 20–25 minutes, stirring constantly in one direction, until the mixture becomes thick and transparent. Add the sugar and boiled water chestnuts, and mix until well blended. Remove from the heat and pour the mixture into small ramekins or molds until $^1/_2$ full. Set aside.
3 Make the Topping by combining all the ingredients in a saucepan and cooking over medium heat for 5–10 minutes, stirring constantly, until the mixture is thickened. Remove from the heat and pour a small amount over the water chestnut mixture in each ramekin or mold. Set aside until the Topping sets.
4 Serve warm or chilled.

Light Butter Cookies

$^1/_2$ cup (1 stick/125 g) butter
$^1/_2$ cup (100 g) sugar
3 egg whites
$^1/_4$ teaspoon vanilla extract
1 cup (150 g) flour

Makes 45 cookies
Preparation time: 30 mins
Cooking time: 7 mins per batch

1 Preheat the oven to 180°C (350°F).
2 Using a mixer set to medium speed, cream the butter and gradually add the sugar. Continue mixing until light and fluffy. Add the egg whites one at a time, beating thoroughly after each egg white is added. Add the vanilla extract.
3 Sift the flour and fold in, blending thoroughly to form a smooth mixture. Spoon the mixture into a pastry bag with a small frosting tip. Pipe 4-in (10-cm) strips of the batter onto greased and floured baking sheets, about 2 in (5 cm) apart. Bake each batch in the preheated oven for about 7 minutes or until the cookies have lightly browned edges.
4 Remove the cookies immediately from the baking sheet to prevent sticking. Transfer to a clean plate and set aside to cool. If not eating immediately, pack in airtight containers.

Sweet Saffron Raisin Rolls

2 cups (300 g) flour, sifted with 1 teaspoon salt
2 teaspoons instant yeast
1 tablespoon fine granulated sugar
$^1/_4$ cup ($^1/_2$ stick/60 g) butter
2 tablespoons yogurt
$^1/_2$ cup (125 ml) warm milk
2 tablespoons raisins
$^1/_4$ teaspoon saffron strands soaked in 2 tablespoons hot milk

Makes 5 pieces
Preparation time: 30 mins
 + 12 hours fermentation
Cooking time: 10 mins

1 Preheat the oven to 480°F (250°C).
2 Combine the flour, yeast, sugar, butter, yogurt and milk in a mixing bowl and knead to form a soft pliable dough. The dough should be fairly sticky.
3 Keep the dough in a deep bowl covered with a plate. Set the dough aside for 12 hours to ferment at room temperature (82°F/28°C). If the dough is fermented on a relatively warm day, you may have to reduce standing time.
4 When the dough is fermented, divide it into 5 portions. Roll each portion out on a floured surface into $^3/_4$-in (2-cm) thick round pieces with the center thinner than the edges and place on a greased baking sheet.
5 Sprinkle the raisins and saffron milk over the dough and bake in the preheated oven for 10 minutes or until golden brown.

Light Coconut Cheesecake

2 cups (400 g) uncooked rice, soaked overnight and then drained
3 eggs
$^1/_2$ cup (100 g) sugar
2 tablespoons melted butter, plus additional for brushing
1 cup (250 ml) thick coconut milk
1 tablespoon baking soda
Banana leaves, for lining
2 cups (240 g) grated cheddar cheese

Makes 2 cakes
Preparation time: **20 mins**
Cooking time: **20 mins**

1 Preheat the oven to 350°F (180°C).

2 Grind the drained rice in a blender or food processor until fine, adding a little water if necessary to keep the mixture turning. Set aside for about 12 hours at room temperature.

3 Beat the eggs in a bowl. Add the sugar and butter and beat until fluffy. Set aside.

4 Pour the thick coconut milk into the ground rice and mix well. Blend the rice mixture with the egg mixture, beating until smooth. Add the baking soda.

5 Line two small baking dishes or heatproof bowls, about 8 in (20 cm) in diameter, with the banana leaves or aluminum foil. Brush the banana leaves or aluminum foil with butter. Pour in the mixture, distributing evenly. Top with the grated cheddar cheese and brush with butter again.

6 Bake in the preheated oven for about 20 minutes or until a knife inserted in the center comes out clean.

Egg and Milk Bonbons

8 egg yolks
1 1/4 cups (300 ml) sweetened condensed milk
1 teaspoon grated lemon rind
1 1/4 cups (250 g) sugar
1/4 teaspoon cream of tartar

Makes about 30 bonbons
Preparation time: 5 mins + 1 3/4 hours
Cooking time: 35 mins

1 Combine the egg yolks and milk in a double boiler. Add the lemon rind. Cook over medium heat, stirring constantly, until very thick and the mixture coats the back of a spoon when lifted, about 20 minutes. Chill for 1 hour for easier handling.

2 Grease your hands and shape the egg mixture into small balls, placing each ball into a greased pan.

3 In a saucepan, melt the sugar and cream of tartar over low heat. Do not stir, otherwise the sugar will crystallize. When the sugar becomes caramelized, stir then dip each ball into the syrup with a pair of tongs, swirling to coat evenly. Keep the syrup over low heat so it does not harden. Alternatively, if you do not wish to coat the bonbons in syrup, dust them lightly with sugar.

4 Put each coated ball into a greased pan and set aside to cool. Wrap individually in plastic wrap, if desired, before serving.

Honey Glazed Bananas

8–10 small ripe bananas
  (about 2–2¹/₂ lbs/
  1–1.25 kg)
¹/₂ cup (125 ml) water
1 cup (250 ml) honey or
  1 cup (200 g) sugar
¹/₂ teaspoon salt

Serves 4–6
Preparation time: 10 mins
Cooking time: 30 mins

1 Peel the bananas and flatten them by gently pressing them with a cutting board or other flat object.
2 Bring the water to a boil in a saucepan. Add the honey or sugar and salt, and boil until the mixture turns into a thin syrup, about 3 minutes. Remove from the heat.
3 Dip the flattened bananas in the syrup and grill on a pan grill over low heat or under a preheated broiler set on low for 5–7 minutes on each side, basting with the syrup occasionally, until golden brown. Remove and serve immediately.

Palm Sugar Barbecued Bananas

Banana "cues" are sold by vendors in the streets of Manila. The glaze adds sweetness, as well as a nice sheen, to the cooked bananas.

$^{1}/_{2}$ cup (125 ml) oil
4 ripe bananas (about
  1 lb/500 g), peeled
$^{1}/_{4}$ cup (50 g) shaved
  palm sugar or dark
  brown sugar
4 bamboo skewers

Serves 4
Preparation time: 5 mins
Cooking time: 10 mins

1 Heat the oil in a wok or large skillet. Add the bananas to the wok, 1–2 at a time. Immediately sprinkle 1 tablespoon palm sugar or brown sugar evenly onto each banana.

2 Cook over low-medium heat until the bananas are tender, about 10 minutes, stirring constantly. The sugar will melt and form a glaze on the bananas as they cook.

3 Thread the bananas onto skewers and transfer to a greased tray. Set aside to cool before serving.

Gulab Jamun

4 cups (1 liter) water
2 cups (400 g) sugar
2 tablespoons rose water
  or 1 teaspoon rose
  extract
$^1/_2$ cup (75 g) self-rising
  flour, sifted
1 teaspoon baking soda
1$^1/_2$ cups (300 g) full
  cream milk powder
$^1/_3$ cup (80 ml) cream or
  evaporated milk
2 teaspoons butter
Oil, for deep-frying

Makes 12
Preparation time: 30 mins
  + 2 hours to soak
Cooking time: 15 mins

1 Bring the water to a boil in a saucepan. Add the sugar and stir until the sugar completely dissolves. Pour in the rose water or extract and mix well. Remove from the heat and set aside.

2 Combine the self-rising flour, baking soda and milk powder in a mixing bowl. Add the cream or evaporated milk, a little at a time and mix the mixture into a thick batter. Lightly grease your hands with butter and knead the mixture into a soft dough. Pinch off a piece of the dough and roll it into a 1-in (2.5-cm) ball. Continue to make the dough balls until all the dough is used up.

3 Heat the oil in a wok or saucepan. Deep-fry the dough balls over low heat, a few at a time and turning them often, until golden brown on all sides, 3–5 minutes. Remove the deep-fried balls from the hot oil with a slotted spoon and drain, then gently drop them into the syrup. Allow to soak in the syrup for 2 hours. Serve warm or at room temperature.

Baked Coconut Slices

1/2 cup (65 g) glutinous rice flour
3/4 cup (135 g) shaved palm sugar or dark brown sugar
2 cups (200 g) grated fresh coconut or 3/4 cup (100 g) dried coconut flakes, soaked in 1 cup (250 ml) water, drained
2 teaspoons pandanus or vanilla extract
2 tablespoons oil

1 Preheat the oven to 400°F (200°C).
2 Combine the glutinous rice flour, palm sugar, coconut and pandanus or vanilla extract in a mixing bowl and mix well.
3 Heat 1 tablespoon of the oil in a wok or saucepan over low heat, turning to grease the sides. Stir-fry the coconut mixture for 20–25 minutes until dry. Remove from the heat.
4 Grease a baking tray with the remaining oil. Pour the cooked coconut mixture into the tray and level it with the back of a wet spoon.
5 Place the tray in the oven and bake for about 10 minutes, until the cake is golden brown on the surface. Cut the cake into the desired shapes and serve warm or at room temperature.

Serves 4–6
Preparation time: **10 mins**
Cooking time: **30 mins**

Sweet Yam Squares

3 purple or red yams
(about 1 lb/500 g)
2 cups (500 ml) water
1 tablespoon melted
butter
1 cup (125 g) rice flour
2 cups (400 g) sugar
1$^1/_4$ cups (300 ml)
cream or evaporated
milk
$^1/_2$ teaspoon vanilla
extract
1 teaspoon baking
soda

Serves 8
Preparation time: **40 mins**
Cooking time: **40 mins**

1 Peel the yams then boil in the water until tender, about 30 minutes. Set aside to cool then grate or mash the yams. Brush a small (6 x 6 in/15 x 15 cm) baking pan with the melted butter.
2 Combine the mashed yam with the rest of the ingredients and stir to mix thoroughly. Pour the mixture into the greased baking pan and steam in a large pot or covered wok for 40 minutes, or until firm.
3 Remove from the heat and set aside to cool for several minutes before serving. Store any leftovers in the refrigerator.

Purple yams are tubers with grayish brown skins and purple flesh tubers. They taste sweet and are sold fresh in Asian grocery stores.

Sticky Rice with Grated Coconut Topping

2 cups (400 g) uncooked glutinous rice, soaked in water overnight to soften, then drained
1 cup (185 g) shaved palm sugar or dark brown sugar
1 teaspoon pandanus or vanilla extract
2$^1/_2$ cups (625 ml) thick coconut milk
$^3/_4$ teaspoon salt
2 tablespoons black and white sesame seeds, pan-roasted for 10 minutes over low heat, to garnish

Grated Coconut Topping
$^1/_3$ cup (80 ml) water
$^1/_2$ cup (100 g) sugar
2 cups (200 g) grated fresh coconut or dried coconut flakes that have been reconstituted by soaking in water, then drained
1 teaspoon pandanus or vanilla extract
$^1/_2$ teaspoon salt

1 To make the Grated Coconut Topping, bring the water to a boil in a saucepan over medium heat. Add the sugar and simmer for 3–5 minutes, stirring constantly, until the sugar completely dissolves and the mixture turns into a thick syrup. Add the grated coconut, fragrant extract and salt, and cook, stirring constantly, for about 7 minutes, adjusting the heat as necessary, until the mixture dries up. Remove and set aside.
2 Line a steamer basket with a cheesecloth and spread the soaked glutinous rice evenly on the cloth. Steam the rice for 15 minutes, then turn it over and steam for 10 more minutes until cooked.
3 Heat the palm sugar, pandanus or vanilla extract, coconut milk and salt in a saucepan over low heat, stirring constantly and taking care not to burn the sugar, until the palm sugar completely dissolves. Remove from the heat and set aside to cool.
4 When the glutinous rice is cooked, transfer to a mixing bowl and smooth the surface with the back of a wet spoon but do not press to pack it. While the rice is still hot, pour the coconut milk mixture over the rice, cover and set aside for 10 minutes, until the mixture is absorbed. Fold the glutinous rice over with a wet spoon to mix thoroughly and set aside.
5 To serve, place several spoonfuls of the glutinous rice in each individual serving bowl and top with the Grated Coconut Topping and a sprinkling of sesame seeds.

Serves 6–8
Preparation time: **30 mins**
Cooking time: **45 mins**

Sticky Rice with Sliced Fresh Mango and Sweet Coconut Sauce

2 cups (400 g) uncooked glutinous rice, soaked in water overnight, then drained
2 teaspoons sesame seeds, pan-roasted for 10 minutes over low heat, to serve
3 ripe mangoes, peeled and sliced

Sweet Coconut Sauce
1 cup (185 g) shaved palm sugar or dark brown sugar
1 teaspoon pandanus or vanilla extract
$2^1/_2$ cups (625 ml) thick coconut milk or cream
$^3/_4$ teaspoon salt

1 Line a steamer basket with a cloth and spread the soaked glutinous rice evenly on the cloth. Steam the rice for 15 minutes, then turn it over and steam for 10 more minutes until cooked.
2 While the rice is being steamed, make the Sweet Coconut Sauce by heating all the ingredients in a saucepan over medium heat for about 5 minutes, stirring constantly, until the sugar completely dissolves. Remove and set aside.
3 When the rice is cooked, transfer to a mixing bowl and smooth the surface with the back of a wet spoon but do not press to pack it. While it is still hot, pour $^3/_4$ of the Sweet Coconut Sauce over the rice, cover with a plate and set aside for 10 minutes, until the Sauce is absorbed. Remove the lid, fold the glutinous rice over with a wet spoon to mix thoroughly. Cover again and set aside.
4 To serve, place small portions of the sticky rice on individual serving plates and drizzle the remaining Sweet Coconut Sauce on top. Serve the sticky rice with a sprinkling of roasted sesame seeds on top and mango slices on the side.

Serves 8 to 10
Preparation time: **15 mins + overnight soaking**
Cooking time: **30 mins**

Fluffy Sweet Rice Cakes

2 cups (400 g) uncooked white rice
1 1/2 cups (375 ml) water
1 tablespoon baking soda
1 cup (200 g) sugar
1/2 teaspoon salt
Banana leaves or aluminum foil for wrapping
2 tablespoons melted butter for brushing
3/4 cup (100 g) grated cheddar cheese

Serves 6
Preparation time: 30 mins
+ 8 hours soaking time
Cooking time: 20–25 mins

1 Soak the rice in the water for 8 hours or overnight. Drain the rice, reserving the liquid. Grind the rice to a smooth paste in a blender, adding a little of the reserved liquid if necessary to keep the mixture turning. It should have the consistency of a dough.
2 Add the baking soda, sugar and salt to the rice dough and mix well.
3 Wilt the banana leaves by passing them over an open flame for a few seconds. Cut the banana leaves or aluminum foil into 4 in (10 cm) circles. Brush with butter and use them to line individual cupcake or muffin molds.
4 Pour the dough into the molds. Steam in a steamer until the cakes are fully cooked, about 20–25 minutes. When the cakes are fully cooked, a knife inserted in the center will come out clean. If desired, top each cake with grated cheddar cheese before serving.

Sticky Rice and Coconut Custard Slices

Bottom Rice Layer

2¹/₄ cups (450 g) uncooked glutinous rice, soaked overnight, drained

1 teaspoon salt

¹/₂ cup (125 ml) thick coconut milk

1 pandanus leaf, tied into a knot

Coconut Custard Topping

5 eggs

1¹/₄ cups (250 g) shaved palm sugar

³/₄ cup (200 ml) thick coconut milk

1 tablespoon rice flour

¹/₄ teaspoon salt

1 To make the Bottom Rice Layer, combine all the ingredients in a 8 in (20 cm) square baking pan. Steam for 30 minutes or until the rice is cooked. Flake the rice with a fork, then press down to compress it. Return to the steamer and steam for another 5 minutes before adding the Custard Topping.

2 Make the Coconut Custard Topping by beating the eggs and sugar in a mixing bowl until the sugar dissolves. Add the rest of the ingredients. Place the mixing bowl over a saucepan of boiling water and heat, stirring all the time until the mixture starts to thicken and coats the back of a spoon. Remove from the heat immediately and pour over the Bottom Rice Layer. Steam over low heat for 25 minutes or until the Custard Topping sets. Cool the cake thoroughly before slicing into desired shapes (cubes or diamonds).

Makes 15–20 pieces
Preparation time: **30 mins**   Cooking time: **1 hour**

Sticky Rice with Durian

$1^1/_2$ cups (300 g) un-
cooked glutinous rice,
soaked overnight,
rinsed and drain
3 cups (750 ml) coconut
cream or thick coconut
milk
$1^1/_2$ cups (300 g) sugar
1 teaspoon salt
1 ripe durian (about
$1^1/_2$ lbs/700 g) opened
and deseeded to yield
about 2 cups of flesh

Serves 4–6
Preparation time: 30
mins + soaking time
Cooking time: 25 mins

1 Line a bamboo steamer with cheesecloth and spread
the rice evenly on it. Steam for 20 minutes, then turn
the rice over and steam for 10 more minutes until
cooked. Transfer to a big bowl and smooth its surface
to level with a wet wooden spoon. Do not pack the rice.
2 Combine the coconut cream, sugar and salt in a bowl.
Stir until the sugar completely dissolves. Set aside.
3 While the rice is still hot, pour $^1/_2$ of the coconut
cream mixture over it and cover with a lid, then set
aside for 10 minutes. Uncover and fold the rice with a
wet wooden spoon from top to bottom to get an even
texture. Cover and set aside again.
4 Add the durian flesh to the bowl of the remaining
coconut cream mixture. Stir to mix well.
5 To serve, portion the rice into serving bowls and
top with the durian coconut cream mixture. Serve
warm or at room temperature.

Sweet Coconut Cream with Corn

1 cup (200 g) uncooked
  glutinous rice
5 cups (1.25 liters) thin
  coconut milk
³/₄ cup (150 g) sugar
1 teaspoon salt
One 15-oz (425-g) can
  whole corn, drained, or
  kernels from 2 fresh
  cobs of corn, steamed
  for 7 minutes
2 cups (500 ml) thick
  coconut milk, to serve

1 Combine the glutinous rice and thin coconut milk in a saucepan. Bring to a boil, then add the sugar, salt and corn kernels.

2 Simmer over very low heat until the rice is tender and the mixture has a porridge-like consistency, about 15 minutes.

3 Pour into individual bowls and serve each bowl with ¹/₄ cup (60 ml) thick coconut milk.

Serves 6–8
Preparation time: **5 mins**
Cooking time: **20 mins**

Coconut Sauce Pancakes

2¹/₂ cups (375 g) flour, sifted
2 eggs, lightly beaten
2 teaspoons instant yeast
1¹/₄ cups (300 ml) warm thick coconut milk
¹/₂ teaspoon vanilla extract
Pinch of salt
1 tablespoon oil or butter

Coconut Sauce

1¹/₂ cups (375 ml) thick coconut milk
1 cup (185 g) shaved palm sugar or dark brown sugar
1–2 tablespoons sugar
Pinch of salt
1 pandanus leaf, raked with a fork and tied into a knot

1 To make the Coconut Sauce, combine all the ingredients in a saucepan and bring to a boil over medium heat, then reduce the heat to low and simmer for 2 more minutes, stirring constantly until the sugar completely dissolves. Remove, discard the pandanus leaf and set aside.

2 Combine the flour, beaten eggs and yeast in a mixing bowl. Gradually stir in the warm thick coconut milk. Add the vanilla extract and salt, and mix into a thick smooth batter. Cover with a cloth and leave the batter to ferment in a warm place for 1 hour. The batter should turn fluffy when it is well fermented.

3 To make the pancakes, lightly grease a small wok or pancake griddle with the oil or butter and heat over low heat. Once the wok or pan is hot, place a ladleful of the batter onto the wok or pan, turning to spread evenly. Cook for about 2–3 minutes until the pancake is set on top, then carefully turn it over with a spatula and cook the other side until golden brown. Remove and set aside. Repeat until all the batter is used up.

4 Pour some Coconut Sauce over each pancake and serve immediately.

Serves 4–6
Preparation time: 20 mins
   + 1 hour fermentation
Cooking time: 30 mins

Combine the batter ingredients to form a thick smooth batter and leave in a warm place to ferment for 1 hour.

Once the pancake sets on top, flip it over to cook the other side until golden brown.

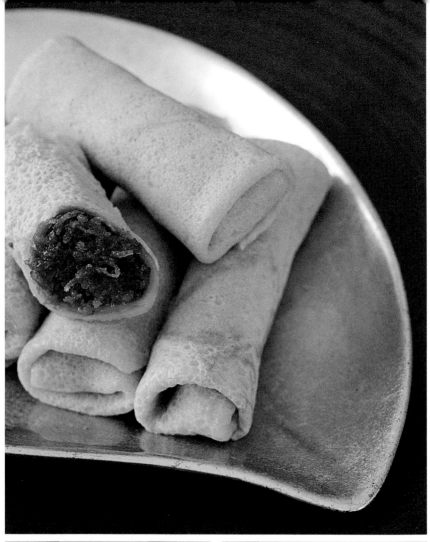

Spoon the Sweet Coconut Pancake Filling into the center of each pancake.

Fold the edges in and roll up each pancake to form parcels.

Sweet Coconut Filled Pancakes

1¹/₄ cups (185 g) flour
¹/₄ teaspoon salt
2 small eggs, beaten
²/₃ cup (150 ml) thin
coconut milk
¹/₂ cup (125 ml) Pandanus
Extract (page 8)
¹/₄ cup (60 ml) water
1 tablespoon oil
1¹/₂ portions Sweet
Coconut Pancake Filling
(page 8)
2 pandanus leaves, fold-
ed in half, loose ends
tied with a rubber band,
looped end snipped to
make a brush
Oil, for greasing pan

Makes 25 pancakes
Preparation time: 1 hour
Cooking time: 15 mins

1 Make the Pandanus Extract and Sweet Coconut Pancake Filling by following the recipes on page 8.
2 Sift the flour and salt into a mixing bowl. Make a well in the center and pour in the eggs, coconut milk and Pandanus Extract. Using a wooden spoon, gradually incorporate the flour into the liquid, making a smooth batter free of lumps. (Strain out any lumps in the batter using a sieve.)
3 Thin the batter with water and stir in the oil. Mix well. Cover the bowl and allow the batter to stand for 20–30 minutes.
4 To cook the pancakes, heat a small skillet or griddle (preferably with a non-stick surface) over medium heat. Dip the pandanus brush in a little oil and lightly brush the pan with it. Ensure that the pan is sufficiently hot (a drop of water should sizzle instantly).
5 Stir the batter. Use a small ladle to pour the batter onto the skillet. Immediately swirl the skillet so that the batter covers the base completely with a thin layer. Allow the batter to set and cook until lightly browned. Flip the pancake and cook the other side for a few seconds.
6 Turn the pancake out onto a plate or tray. Repeat with the remaining batter, stacking the finished pancakes on a plate. If the batter starts to thicken, add 1–2 tablespoons of water.
7 Place a spoonful of the Sweet Coconut Pancake Filling in the center of each pancake, fold both sides towards the middle over the filling and roll the pancake up, neatly enclosing the filling and creating a little parcel.

Coconut Patties with Palm Sugar Syrup

1 tablespoon cooked rice blended with 1 cup (250 ml) warm water until smooth
1¹/₂ cups (185 g) rice flour
1 teaspoon instant yeast
2 teaspoons sugar
¹/₄ teaspoon salt
1¹/₂ cups (375 ml) thick coconut milk
Oil, for greasing pan
1 portion Palm Sugar Syrup (page 7), for serving

Serves 4
Preparation time: 20 mins + fermentation and standing time
Cooking time: 15 mins

1 Mix the rice mixture, rice flour, yeast, sugar and salt in a mixing bowl until it forms a thick, smooth batter. Cover and set aside for 4 hours to ferment at room temperature (82°F/28°C). On a warm day, you may have to reduce the fermentation time.
2 Add the coconut milk and mix to form a slightly watery batter. Set aside for 2 hours.
3 Heat a small wok or skillet and grease it lightly with oil.
4 Pour 3–4 tablespoons of the batter into the wok and swirl the wok gently so that about 1¹/₄ in (3 cm) of the side of the wok is thinly coated and the remaining batter collects at the center. Care should be taken that it is rotated only twice. Cover with a tight-fitting lid.
5 Reduce the heat to low and cook for about 3 minutes until set so the edges resemble crisp lace, the center is soft and well-risen, and the bottom is golden brown. Serve with Palm Sugar Syrup.

Tropical Bread Pudding

1 tablespoon softened
   butter
2 eggs
$^1/_3$ cup (70 g) sugar
$^3/_4$ cup (190 ml) thick
   coconut milk
$^2/_3$ cup (150 ml) milk
Few drops vanilla extract
6 slices white bread, cut
   into $1^1/_4$-in (3-cm)
   squares
$^1/_3$ cup (50 g) raisins
Extra sugar, for sprinkling

1 Preheat the oven to 350°F (180°C).

2 Lightly brush the base and sides of a shallow 6-in (15-cm) heatproof baking dish with the softened butter; set aside.

3 In a bowl, beat the eggs and sugar together and pour in the coconut milk and milk. Flavor with a few drops of vanilla extract. Add the bread and raisins and set aside for 20–30 minutes, stirring occasionally to ensure even soaking.

4 Turn the mixture out into the buttered container and spread out evenly. Sprinkle a tablespoon of the sugar on the top and bake for 30–40 minutes or until golden brown. Cool before cutting into $1^1/_4$-in (3-cm) squares for serving.

Serves 4–6
Preparation time: **15 mins + 30 mins soaking time**
Cooking time: **40 mins**

Banana Custard Surprise

1¹/₄ cups (160 g) rice flour
2 tablespoons tapioca flour or cornstarch
2 cups (500 ml) thin coconut milk
¹/₂ cup (100 g) sugar
Pinch of salt
2 pandanus leaves, torn lengthwise and tied into a knot
2–3 ripe bananas (about 13 oz/375g), sliced into 16 diagonal pieces
2–3 sheets banana leaves, softened and cut into 16 squares measuring 7 x 7 in (18 x 18 cm)

Makes 16 parcels
Preparation time: **30 mins**
Cooking time: **30 mins**

1 Place the rice flour and tapioca flour into a bowl and mix with ³/₄ cup (190 ml) of the coconut milk, stirring well to remove any lumps. Set aside.
2 Pour the remaining coconut milk into a saucepan with the sugar, salt and pandanus leaves. Bring to a boil over medium heat. When the coconut milk comes to a boil, pour in the flour mixture, stirring continuously with a wooden spoon to make a thick, smooth custard.
3 Spoon 2 tablespoons of the custard mixture onto each banana leaf square or aluminum foil. Place a slice of banana on top of the custard, then spoon another 2 tablespoons of custard mixture onto the banana to enclose it.
4 Shape the custard into an oblong roll and fold the banana leaf around it. Fold both ends under to make a 2¹/₂ x 3¹/₄ in (6 x 8 cm) packet. Arrange the packets in a steamer and steam for 20 minutes. Set aside to cool before serving.

Banana leaves should be scalded by pouring boiling water over them in a tub or basin and letting them soak for a minute until they just begin to soften, so they do not crack when folded. They are sold fresh in rectangular sheets in markets. If banana leaves are not available, substitute aluminum foil.

Enclose the banana slice in the rice custard.

Shape the filling into an oblong roll, then fold the leaf around it and fold the ends under it.

Sago Pudding with Melon Balls

1 ripe cantaloupe or
   honeydew melon
3 cups (750 ml) water
$^1/_2$ cup (75 g) dried sago
   pearls
$^1/_2$ cup (100 g) sugar
1 cup (250 ml) coconut
   cream or thick coconut
   milk combined with
   1 teaspoon salt
1 portion Palm Sugar
   Syrup (page 7)

Serves 4–6
Preparation time: 25 mins
Cooking time: 30 mins

1 Cut the melon in half and scrape out the seeds. With a melon baller, scoop out round balls and place them in the refrigerator to chill.
2 Bring the water to a boil in a pot or saucepan over medium heat. Add the sago pearls and cook, stirring occasionally, until the pearls are almost clear, with tiny white spots in the center, about 7–10 minutes. Add the sugar and stir until the sugar completely dissolves. Remove from the heat and refrigerate to chill.
3 Make the Palm Sugar Syrup by following the recipe on page 7.
4 To serve, portion the chilled sago pudding into serving bowls. Drizzle with the Palm Sugar Syrup and top with the melon balls. Spoon the coconut cream mixture on top and serve chilled.

Coconut Caramel Flan

Caramel

$^3/_4$ cup (150 g) sugar

4 tablespoons water or young coconut juice

Coconut Custard

3 cups (750 ml) coconut cream or thick coconut milk

$^1/_3$ cup (65 g) sugar

4 eggs, gently beaten

$^1/_2$ teaspoon vanilla extract

$^3/_4$ cup (125 g) fresh or canned young coconut

Serves 4–6

Preparation time: **20 mins**

Cooking time: **45 mins**

1 To make the Caramel, bring the sugar and water or coconut juice to a boil in a saucepan over medium heat, without stirring. Cook until the sugar turns golden brown. Remove from the heat and pour the Caramel syrup into 4 ovenproof bowls. Set aside.

2 Preheat the oven to 325°F (160°C).

3 Make the Coconjut Custard by gently heating the coconut cream and sugar in a saucepan over medium heat until warm. Do not boil. Remove from the heat and stir to dissolve the sugar. Gradually stir in the egg and vanilla extract.

4 Strain the mixture and add the coconut meat. Pour the mixture into the bowls containing the Caramel syrup. Place the bowls in a baking dish half-filled with boiling water and bake in the oven until set, about 25–35 minutes. Remove from the oven, set aside to cool and chill in the refrigerator. Served the chilled caramel in the bowls or inverted onto serving plates as shown.

Ginger Crème Brulée

This is a Vietnamese version of the popular French crème brulée, flavored with fresh ginger rather than the traditional vanilla bean. A chilled custard of pure cream is covered with a thin crust of crunchy glazed sugar.

2 cups (500 ml) cream
2$^1/_2$ in (6 cm) fresh ginger, peeled, then halved and bruised
3 egg yolks
$^1/_4$ cup (50 g) fine granulated sugar
4 ovenproof bowls (each 4 in/10 cm in diameter)
1 large baking pan (to hold the 4 bowls)
4 tablespoons sugar

Serves 4
Preparation time: 15 mins + 15 mins standing + 2 hours chilling
Cooking time: 35 mins

1 Heat the cream and ginger in a saucepan over low heat, stirring from time to time, until the mixture almost comes to a boil. Remove from the heat, cover the pan and set aside for 15 minutes. Remove and discard the ginger pieces.

2 Preheat the oven to 350°F (180°C).

3 Mix the egg yolks and sugar in a large bowl until the sugar completely dissolves, then gradually pour in the ginger-flavored cream, whisking to mix well. Do not beat the cream as this will cause air bubbles in the custard.

4 Pour the custard mixture into the 4 ovenproof bowls and place them in a deep baking pan. Carefully fill the baking pan with boiling water up to half the height of the bowls, then bake in the oven until the cream just sets in the middle, 30–35 minutes. Remove and set aside to cool. When the custard is cool enough, chill in the refrigerator for at least 1 hour.

5 Sprinkle the top of each custard with 1 tablespoon of the sugar and grill under a preheated broiler for about 1 minute, until the sugar blisters and turns golden brown. (Alternatively, you may sear the surface of the custard using a torch.) Remove and set aside to cool.

6 Return the custard to the refrigerator and chill for at least 1 hour before serving.

Sweet Corn Puddings in Banana Leaf Cups

1 ear fresh corn or 1 cup (150 g) canned or frozen corn kernels
$^1/_2$ cup (65 g) rice flour
2 cups (500 ml) water
1 teaspoon pandanus or vanilla extract
1 cup (200 g) sugar
40 banana leaf cups made from 10 to 12 banana leaf sheets or aluminum foil (see step-by-step below) or cupcake ramekins

Topping
$^1/_3$ cup (40 g) rice flour
$1^1/_2$ cups (375 ml) thick coconut milk
$^1/_4$ cup (50 g) sugar
$^3/_4$ teaspoon salt

1 If using fresh corn, husk it and cut the kernels from the cobs with a knife to yield about 1 cup. In a saucepan or small pot, boil the corn kernels in $1^1/_2$ cups (375 ml) of water for 2–3 minutes until soft. Remove and drain.

2 Combine the rice flour, water and pandanus or vanilla extract in a saucepan and mix well. Cook over medium heat for 20–25 minutes, stirring continuously in one direction with a wooden spoon, until the mixture is thick and transparent. Add the sugar and corn, mix until the sugar completely dissolves. Remove from the heat.

3 While the corn mixture is still warm and fluid, spoon it into the banana leaf cups or ramekins until they are all $^2/_3$ full and set aside.

4 To make the Topping, combine all the ingredients in a saucepan and cook over medium heat for about 10 minutes, stirring constantly, until the mixture thickens. Remove from the heat.

5 While the Topping is still warm, spoon it over the corn mixture to fill each cup or ramekin. Set aside until the Topping sets. Serve chilled or at room temperature.

Makes 40 cups
Preparation time: **1 hour**
Cooking time: **30 mins**

Cut out 80 leaf squares, each 4 in (10 cm) across. Stack 2 squares to make each cup.

On each side, make a cut ($^3/_4$ in/2 cm deep) about $^3/_4$ in (2 cm) from the edge.

Fold up the sides of the squares and staple the overlapping corners to fasten.

Repeat with the remaining 2 corners to fold the squares into a cup.

Sweet Coconut Pumpkin Custard

1 small pumpkin (about
  1 lb/500 g)
5 eggs
$^1/_4$ cup (90 g) shaved
  palm sugar or dark
  brown sugar
$^1/_2$ teaspoon salt
1 cup (250 ml) thick
  coconut milk

Serves 4–6
Preparation time: 30 mins
Cooking time: 40 mins

1 Carefully cut out a 2-in (5-cm) section around the stem of the pumpkin and lift it out to form the "lid." Scoop out the seeds.
2 Lightly beat the eggs in a mixing bowl. Add the palm sugar, salt and coconut milk. Stir until the sugar completely dissolves and the mixture is well blended.
3 Pour the mixture into the pumpkin. Replace the "lid" and steam the whole pumpkin in a steamer for 20–30 minutes over high heat, until the custard is set. Remove and set aside to cool.
4 Slice the pumpkin into wedges and serve warm or chilled.

Mango Pudding with Whipped Cream

3 large ripe mangoes
  (about 3 lbs/1.5 kg)
2¹/₂ tablespoons gelatin
  powder
¹/₂ cup (125 ml) cold
  water
¹/₂ cup (125 ml) boiling
  water
³/₄ cup (150 g) sugar
³/₄ cup (190 ml) cream
  or evaporated milk
1 teaspoon vanilla extract
Whipped cream, for top-
  ping (optional)
1 small ripe mango,
  sliced into wedges, for
  topping (optional)

1 Peel and slice the mangoes and purée the flesh in a blender. Soften the gelatin powder in the cold water, then stir in the boiling water and continue stirring until the gelatin completely dissolves. Set aside to cool. Combine the gelatin and mango purée and mix thoroughly.

2 Stir the sugar and cream or evaporated milk in a bowl until the sugar completely dissolves. Add to the mango-gelatin mixture. Stir in the vanilla extract.

3 Pour the mixture into 6 dessert bowls and chill for 6 hours, or until firm.

4 Top with whipped cream and mango wedges, if desired, before serving.

Serves 6
Preparation time: 15 mins
Setting time: 6 hours

Mini Custard Flans

$^3/_4$ cup (150 g) sugar
$^1/_4$ teaspoon cream of
tartar
1 teaspoon grated lemon
rind, to serve (optional)
Whipped cream, to serve
(optional)

Custard Mixture

1 cup (200 g) sugar
5 egg yolks
1 egg
1 teaspoon grated lemon
rind
$^1/_2$ teaspoon vanilla extract

Serves 4
Preparation time: 20 mins
Cooking time: 20 mins

1 Heat the sugar and cream of tartar in a saucepan over low heat, without stirring, until the sugar melts and forms a thin brown syrup, 15–20 minutes.
2 Remove from the heat. Divide the mixture into 4 portions and spoon just enough of the sugar mixture to cover the bottom of each muffin cup or flan mold. Let stand until the sugar hardens, about 1 minute.
3 To make the Custard Mixture, whip the sugar, egg yolks and egg together. Strain into a bowl. Add the lemon rind and vanilla extract and blend well. Set aside.
4 Divide the Custard Mixture into 4 portions and pour each portion over the hardened sugar mixture. Place the cups or molds in a steamer and steam for 10 minutes, or until firm, making sure the water does not enter the molds.
5 Remove from the heat and set aside to cool slightly. Run a knife gently around the edges of the molds to loosen the flans. Invert onto a serving platter. Serve with lemon rind and whipped cream if desired.

Banana Fritters

10 ripe bananas (about
2¹/₂ lbs/1.25 kg),
peeled and sliced in
half lengthwise
Oil, for deep-frying

Batter
³/₄ cup (100 g) rice flour
¹/₃ cup (50 g) flour
¹/₂ teaspoon salt
¹/₂ teaspoon sugar
²/₃ cup (150 ml) water

Serves 4
Preparation time: 20 mins
Cooking time: 20 mins

1 To make the Batter, combine both flour in a small mixing bowl. Add the salt, sugar and all but 2 tablespoons of the water. Stir until free from lumps; the Batter should coat the back of a spoon thinly (add more water if needed).
2 Pour the oil into a pan or wok to a depth of 1¹/₄ in (3 cm) and heat over medium heat.
3 Working with a few pieces at a time, dip the banana slices into the Batter to coat thoroughly and then gently lower into the hot oil and fry until golden brown, about 3–4 minutes. Remove from the oil and drain on paper towels. Serve warm.

Sweet potato, jackfruit or yam fritters can also be made using this recipe. Peel 2 small sweet potatoes or 1 medium yam and cut into ¹/₄-in (6-mm) slices. Dip in the Batter and fry in hot oil until golden brown.

Sweet Potato Doughnuts

2 medium sweet potatoes or yams (about 350 g/12 oz)

$^1/_2$ cup (75 g) flour

$^1/_2$ teaspoon baking soda

Oil for deep-frying

Fine granulated sugar, for dredging

It is imperative that the temperature of the oil is kept low (the doughnuts should sizzle slightly upon contact with the oil). Frying doughnuts at too high a temperature will result in an unattractive, blistered appearance.

Makes about 12 doughnuts

Preparation time: 40 mins

Cooking time: 40 mins

1 Scrub the sweet potatoes clean under running water. Place in a pan and cover with water. Boil until tender—test by inserting a skewer into the thickest part of the potato; it should go in easily. Remove the sweet potatoes from the water and set aside.

2 When cool enough to handle, peel the skins. Mash the sweet potatoes until free of lumps. Discard any tough fibers.

3 Sift the flour and baking soda together and add to the mashed potatoes, kneading lightly until smooth.

4 Break off small pieces of the dough about the size of a small lime (about 1 oz/30 g each) and roll into smooth balls, flouring your hands lightly to prevent the dough from sticking. Flatten the balls slightly and make a hole through the center of each one with the floured handle of a wooden spoon. Smoothen the edges around the hole with your fingers. Repeat until the dough is used up. Lay the doughnuts on a lightly-floured tray or cloth as you shape them.

5 Heat the oil in a pan or wok over medium heat. The oil should be about 1 in (2.5 cm) deep. Reduce the heat to low and fry the doughnuts until golden brown, 3–4 minutes on each side. Drain on paper towels.

6 Dredge the doughnuts in the sugar and serve.

Peel and mash the sweet potatoes until free of lumps.

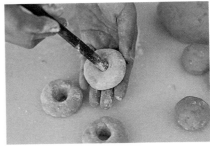

Pierce the center of each flattened ball with the floured handle of a wooden spoon.

Quick Jelly Rolls

4 eggs
1 cup (200 g) sugar
1 cup (150 g) flour
1 teaspoon baking soda
1/2 teaspoon salt
1/4 cup (1/2 stick/60 g) butter, melted
Icing sugar, for dusting
1/2 cup (125 ml) strawberry or raspberry jam

Serves 8–10
Preparation time: 20 mins
Cooking time: 20 mins

1 Preheat the oven to 350°F (180°C).
2 Beat the eggs until bright yellow and thick. Gradually stir in the sugar. Sift the flour, baking soda and salt into the egg mixture.
3 Scoop out one cup of the egg-flour mixture and fold into the butter. Fold back into the egg-flour mixture.
4 Pour the mixture into a baking sheet lined with greaseproof paper. Bake in the preheated oven for 20 minutes.
5 Sprinkle the icing sugar onto a piece of greaseproof paper. Invert the sponge cake onto the paper, then peel off the top sheet of greaseproof paper. Invert again into the greaseproof paper. Set aside to cool.
6 When cooled, spread the jam on top of the sponge cake, then roll tightly. Dust the roll with the icing sugar. Cut into thin slices to serve.

Sift the flour, baking soda and salt into the egg mixture.

Invert the sponge cake onto a piece of greaseproof paper sprinkled with icing sugar.

Peel off the top layer of greaseproof paper.

When cooled, spread the jam on the top of the sponge cake then roll tightly.

Frozen Tropical Fruit Salad

A favorite at parties and during the holiday season, this frozen treat combines fresh fruits with a sweet, creamy sauce. Make sure you thaw it in the refrigerator for 1–2 hours before serving.

1 cup (250 ml) thick whipping cream
$^1/_2$ cup (125 g) cream cheese, softened
$^3/_4$ cup (190 ml) sweetened condensed milk
4 cups (500 g) mixed fresh fruits (pineapple, mango, papaya, lychees, bananas), cut into bite-sized pieces

1 Whip the cream until fluffy. Add the cream cheese and condensed milk then whip until smooth. Fold in the fresh fruits and transfer to a large bowl and cover.
2 Freeze for about 8 hours or until firm. Thaw about 30 minutes in the refrigerator before serving.

Serves 6–8
Preparation time: 15 mins + 30 mins thawing
Freezing time: 8 hours

Sweet Stewed Bananas

8 ripe bananas (approx
2 lbs/1 kg), peeled
1³/₄ cups (325 g) shaved
palm sugar or dark
brown sugar
4 cups (1 liter) water
1 teaspoon vanilla extract
2 cups (500 ml) fresh
cream, evaporated milk
or coconut cream
Crushed ice

Serves 8–10
Preparation time: **5 mins**
Cooking time: **50 mins**

1 Slice each banana diagonally into bite-sized pieces.
2 Combine the palm sugar or dark brown sugar and
water in a casserole dish or pot. Bring to a boil, stirring
occasionally until the sugar completely dissolves.
3 Add the bananas and return to a boil. Lower the
heat and simmer until the bananas are tender and the
liquid becomes thick and syrupy, about 40 minutes.
Skim and discard any impurities that rise to the top.
4 Stir in the vanilla extract and set aside to cool.
5 Spoon the bananas and syrup into individual serving
bowls. Add ¹/₄ cup (60 ml) fresh cream, evaporated
milk or coconut cream to each serving. Top with the
crushed ice and serve.

Bananas in Sweet Coconut Milk

6 ripe bananas (about 1²/₃ lbs/750 g), peeled,
1 cup (250 ml) water
2 cups (500 ml) thick coconut milk
1 pandanus leaf, washed and tied into a knot, or few drops pandanus or vanilla extract (optional)
¹/₂ cup (100 g) sugar
¹/₄ teaspoon salt (optional)
3 tablespoons dried sago pearls, rinsed and drained
4 tablespoons sesame seeds, dry-roasted in a skillet for 10 minutes over low heat until browned

1 Slice each banana in half lengthwise. Slice each half into 3 pieces, to obtain a total of 36 pieces

2 Combine the water, coconut milk, pandanus leaf or extract, sugar and salt (if using) in a large saucepan and cook over medium heat, stirring constantly, until the sugar completely dissolves. Reduce the heat to low, add the sago pearls, cover and simmer over low heat for 5–7 minutes, stirring occasionally, until the sago pearls are half cooked. Add the bananas and simmer uncovered for another 5–7 minutes, stirring from time to time, until the sago pearls turn translucent. Remove from the heat.

3 Serve cold or hot in individual serving bowls with a sprinkling of sesame seeds on top.

Serves 4–6
Preparation time: **15 mins**
Cooking time: **10 mins**

Bananas with Iced Coconut Custard

5 ripe bananas (about
  1 1/3 lbs/625 g)
  steamed until soft,
  about 6 minutes
3–5 cups crushed ice

Coconut Custard
3/4 cup (100 g) rice flour
4 cups (1 liter) thick
  coconut milk
2 pandanus leaves, tied
  into a knot
1/4 teaspoon salt
3/4 cup (150 g) sugar
1/2 teaspoon vanilla extract

Syrup
1/2 cup (125 ml) water
1/2 cup (100 g) sugar

1 To make the Coconut Custard, mix the rice flour with 1/2 cup (125 ml) of the coconut milk. Set aside.
2 Bring the rest of the coconut milk, pandanus leaves and salt to a boil in a saucepan, stirring constantly. Simmer for 2 minutes. Remove and discard the pandanus leaves. Stir in the rice flour mixture and simmer until the mixture thickens to a custard, about 2 minutes. Add the sugar and vanilla extract, and stir until the sugar completely dissolves. Set aside to cool.
3 Make the Syrup by bringing the water and sugar to a boil in a small saucepan, stirring constantly. Simmer uncovered for 3 minutes and set aside to cool.
4 Peel the bananas and slice. Divide into 4–6 serving bowls. Add some of the Coconut Custard and about 1/2 cup crushed ice to each bowl. Top each portion with some Syrup and serve immediately.

Serves 4–6
Preparation time: **20 mins**   Cooking time: **25 mins**

Sago Pearls with Melon Balls and Coconut Cream

1 1/2 cups (375 ml) water
1/2 cup (75 g) dried sago pearls
1 cup (250 ml) coconut juice
1/2 cup (100 g) flesh of young coconut
1/3 cup (65 g) sugar
1/2 cup (125 ml) thick coconut milk
1/4 teapoon salt
1/2 cantaloupe, flesh scooped with melon baller

1 Bring the water to a boil in a saucepan. Add the sago pearls and coconut juice. Return to a boil. Reduce the heat to medium and simmer, stirring constantly, until the pearls are soft and translucent, 5–7 minutes. Stir in the coconut meat and sugar, and simmer for 3–5 more minutes, until the sugar completely dissolves. Remove from the heat.

2 In a small saucepan, heat the coconut milk over low heat until warm. Do not allow it to boil. Add the salt, mix well and remove from the heat.

3 Spoon the dessert into individual serving bowls and top each bowl with a few melon balls and 2 table-spoons of the coconut milk. Serve warm or chilled.

Serves 4–6
Preparation time: **10 mins**
Cooking time: **15 mins**

Homemade Coconut Ice Cream

$^1/_2$ cup (125 ml) water
1 cup (200 g) sugar
3$^1/_2$ cups (875 ml) thick
  coconut milk
Mixed fruits of your
  choice (jackfruit, young
  coconut flesh, water-
  melon, lychees), diced
  to yield 2 cups (optional)

Serves 6 to 8
Preparation time: 30 mins
  + 2 to 3 hours freezing
Cooking time: 15 mins

1 Bring the water and sugar to a boil in a saucepan over medium heat, stirring until the sugar completely dissolves and the mixture thickens into a thick syrup. Remove from the heat and set aside to cool. When the syrup is lukewarm, add the coconut milk and mix well.
2 Pour the mixture into a metal mixing bowl and place in the freezer until it is firm around the edges, but still slushy in the middle, about 45 minutes.
3 Remove from the freezer and beat the mixture with a wooden spoon or electric mixer, then chill the mixture in the freezer until it is again firm around the edges. Repeat this process a few more times until the ice cream is uniformly frozen. Allow the ice cream to soften slightly in the refrigerator before serving. Alternatively, pour the mixture into an ice cream maker and freeze according to manufacturer's directions.
4 To serve, place the mixed fruits (if using) in individual serving bowls and top with the coconut ice cream.

Sago and Honeydew Melon in Coconut Milk

4 cups (1 liter) water
3 tablespoons dried sago
  pearls
2 cups (500 ml) thin
  coconut milk
$^1/_2$ cup (100 g) sugar
1 pandanus leaf, tied into
  a knot
$^1/_2$ ripe honeydew melon,
  peeled and diced to
  yield 3 cups (500 g)
Ice cubes

Serves 5–6
Preparation time: **30 mins**
Assembling time: **20 mins**

1 Bring the water to a boil in a large pan. Add the sago and stir to keep the grains moving and prevent them from settling to the bottom of the pan. Cook the sago for 5 minutes. Turn off the heat, cover the pan and set aside for 10 minutes.
2 Pour the sago into a strainer and rinse under running water to wash off the excess starch. Leave the sago in the sieve to drain thoroughly.
3 Place the coconut milk, sugar and pandanus leaf in a pan and heat gently to a boiling point. Remove from the heat and set it in a sink of cold water to cool. When the coconut milk reaches room temperature, pour into a jug and refrigerate until ready to serve.
4 To serve, place a spoonful of the sago and diced honeydew melon in a bowl and pour over some sweetened coconut milk. Add ice cubes and serve immediately.

Sweet Pearl Barley with Ginkgo Nuts

$^1/_4$ cup (50 g) pearl barley, rinsed in several changes of water until the water runs clear, drained
$6^1/_4$ cups (1.5 liters) water
2 cups (200 g) ginkgo nuts (with shells)
1 pandanus leaf, tied into a knot
$^1/_2$ cup (120 g) or more rock sugar, or sugar

Serves 4–6
Preparation time: 20 mins
Soaking time: 20 mins
Cooking time: 1 hour
  15 mins

1 Place the barley in a medium saucepan with the water and leave to soak for 20 minutes.
2 Carefully crack the ginkgo nut shells and remove the nuts. Place in a small pan, cover with water and bring to a boil. Remove the pan from the heat, drain the water and run cold water over the nuts—this makes it easier to peel off the papery skins covering the nuts. There is also a germ within the ginkgo nuts which needs to be removed as it is bitter. You can do this by either splitting the nut into half and removing it, or by gently pushing it out using a toothpick.
3 Place the ginkgo nuts into the saucepan with the soaked barley and bring to a boil. Simmer until tender, about 45 minutes, adding the pandanus leaf halfway through the cooking.
4 Remove the pandanus leaf and sweeten to taste. Serve either warm or cold.

Sweet Black Rice Pudding

³/₄ cup (150 g) uncooked black glutinous rice (*pulut hitam*)
4 cups (1 liter) water
1 pandanus leaf, tied into a knot
¹/₂ cup (100 g) or slightly more sugar (depending on sweetness desired)
1 cup (250 ml) thick coconut milk
¹/₄ teaspoon salt

Serves 4–6
Preparation time: 40 mins
Cooking time: 1 hour 10 mins

1 Pick the rice over for husks and any foreign particles. Wash in several changes of water and then cover with fresh water. Leave to soak for 30 minutes.
2 Drain the rice and add 4 cups (1 liter) fresh water. Bring to a boil together with the pandanus leaf; then reduce the heat to low and simmer until the grains are soft and most of the liquid has evaporated, about 1 hour. (The final consistency should be creamy and porridge-like; if it looks dry, add more water.)
3 Add the sugar and cook for another 10 minutes then remove from the heat.
4 Combine the coconut milk and salt in a small pan. Heat gently, stirring constantly, until it reaches boiling point. Remove immediately from the heat. Serve the porridge in small bowls with a spoonful of coconut milk swirled on the top.

Sweet Red Bean Soup

$^3/_4$ cup (150 g) dried azuki beans (red beans), picked clean, rinsed and drained
$^1/_2$-in (12-mm) piece dried tangerine peel, washed and soaked in $^1/_4$ cup (60 ml) hot water
7 cups (1.75 liters) water
$^1/_2$ cup (100 g) sugar
1 tablespoon cornstarch dissolved in 2 tablespoons water (optional)

1 Put the azuki beans, dried tangerine peel and water in a 3-liter saucepan. Bring to a boil.
2 Reduce the heat, cover and simmer over low heat for 1 hour until softened.
3 Add the sugar and stir. Trickle the cornstarch mixture into the soup to thicken the consistency, if desired.

Azuki beans are small red beans that are boiled until soft and eaten whole in desserts. They are also boiled and mashed to make sweet red bean paste, a filling used in many Japanese cakes and desserts. They may be substituted with red kidney beans.

Serves 4
Preparation time: **20 mins**
Cooking time: **1 hour**

Coconut Mung Bean Dessert

1 cup (200 g) dried mung beans, rinsed and drained
6 cups (1.5 liters) water
2 pandanus leaves, or 2 drops Pandanus Extract (page 8)
1¹/₂ tablespoons dried sago pearls (optional)
4 tablespoons coconut cream or thick coconut milk
¹/₄ teaspoon salt
³/₄ cup (135 g) shaved palm sugar or dark brown sugar
1–3 tablespoons sugar

1 Place the beans and water in a saucepan and set aside to soak for 30 minutes.

2 Rake the pandanus leaves with a fork and tie into a knot. Add the pandanus leaves or Pandanus Extract to the pan and bring to a boil. Then reduce the heat to low, cover and simmer for 45 minutes until the beans are soft.

3 If using the sago, rinse it first under cold running water, then add it to the saucepan. Continue to simmer, uncovered, stirring occasionally for 15 minutes.

4 Discard the pandanus leaves. Add the coconut cream, salt, palm sugar and sugar. Cook, stirring gently, for 1–2 minutes. Serve warm or chilled.

Serves 4
Preparation time: **40 mins**
Cooking time: **1 hour**

Sweet Pumpkin in Coconut Syrup

1¼ lbs (600 g) pumpkin
2 pandanus leaves, or
  2 drops Pandanus
  Extract (page 8)
1 cup (185 g) shaved
  palm sugar or dark
  brown sugar
2 cups (500 ml) thick
  coconut milk
¾ teaspoon salt

Serves 4
Preparation time: **10 mins**
Cooking time: **20 mins**

1 Peel the pumpkin and cut into bite-sized chunks. Set aside. Rake the pandanus leaves with a fork, if using, then tie into a knot.

2 Heat the palm sugar, coconut milk, pandanus leaves or Pandanus Extract, and salt in a pan over low heat, stirring constantly to prevent the coconut milk from separating.

3 When the palm sugar has dissolved, add the pumpkin and cook, uncovered, stirring gently until the pumpkin is tender but not mushy, about 15 minutes. Discard the pandanus leaves if using. Serve warm or at room temperature.

Chendol (Sweet Jellies in Iced Coconut Milk)

Shaved ice or ice cubes, to serve

2 cups (500 ml) thick coconut milk

Pandanus Extract
10 pandanus leaves, rinsed and cut into short lengths
3/4 cup (190 ml) water

Chendol Jellies
6 tablespoons green pea flour (see note)
2 tablespoons rice flour

Palm Sugar Syrup
2/3 cup (150 ml) water
1 cup (185 g) shaved palm sugar or dark brown sugar

Serves 4
Preparation time: 40 mins
Cooking time: 20 mins

1 To make the Pandanus Extract, blend the pandanus leaves with the water in a blender until liquidized. Strain through a sieve and squeeze the pulp to obtain the Pandanus Extract. Discard the solids.

2 To make the Chendol Jellies, pour the Pandanus Extract into a measuring jug and top up with water to make 2 cups (500 ml) of liquid. Add the green pea flour and rice flour. Stir well until free from lumps, then strain this mixture into a pan. Cook over medium heat, stirring continuously, until the mixture boils and thickens, about 5 minutes.

3 Remove the pan from the heat and form the mixture into little strands (see note). If using a perforated ladle, hold it over a bowl of ice water and, working with a spoonful of mixture at a time, pass it through the holes in the ladle by pressing on the mixture with a spoon or rubber spatula. The mixture should pass through in little strands. Remember to work fairly quickly as you must shape the Chendol Jellies while the mixture is still very warm. Once it cools, it will set and become difficult to press through the ladle.

4 To make the Palm Sugar Syrup, place the water and palm sugar in a saucepan. Bring to a boil, then reduce the heat and simmer over medium heat until the sugar completely dissolves and the mixture becomes syrupy. Set aside to cool, then strain into a bowl.

5 To serve, place 2–3 tablespoons of Chendol Jellies in a bowl and top with plenty of shaved ice or 5–6 ice cubes. Add about 1/2 cup (125 ml) of thick coconut milk and drizzle 1–2 spoonfuls of Palm Sugar Syrup to sweeten. Serve immediately.

Traditionally, the cooked *chendol* mixture is passed through a frame with round holes, but if you don't own a *chendol*-making frame, you can improvize by using a perforated ladle.

Sweet Mung Bean Pudding

1 cup (250 g) dried split
  yellow mung beans,
  soaked in water for
  4 hours
1¹/₂ cups (300 g) sugar
1 cup (250 ml) water
2 tablespoons cornstarch
  mixed with 3 table-
  spoons cold water
1 cup (250 ml) coconut
  cream combined with
  1 teaspoon salt

Serves 4–6
Preparation time: 10 mins
  + soaking time
Cooking time: 30 mins

1 Place the mung beans in a pot of water and boil
until they are soft enough to be mashed between your
fingers, about 20 minutes without presoaking, or less
time with presoaking. Do not overcook until they are
falling apart. Drain and set aside.
2 Combine the sugar and water in a saucepan over
medium heat and cook until the sugar completely
dissolves and turn into a thin syrup, 3–5 minutes.
Add the cooked mung beans and stir to mix well.
3 Stir in the cornstarch mixture and cook until the
cornstarch is clear and the mung bean mixture
thickens, 3–5 minutes. Remove from the heat.
4 To serve, divide the pudding into individual serving
bowls and drizzle with the coconut cream and salt
mixture. Serve warm.

Banana and Sago Pearls in Coconut Cream

6 bananas (about 1^2/$_3$ lbs/ 750 g)
1^1/$_2$ teaspoons salt
4 cups (1 liter) water
^{3}/$_4$ cup (110 g) dried sago pearls
^{3}/$_4$ cup (150 g) sugar or more to taste
2 cups (500 ml) coconut cream
1 teaspoon pandanus or vanilla extract

Serves 4–6
Preparation time: 10 mins
Cooking time: 30 mins

1 Select bananas that are not fully ripe; pick those with greenish skins. Ripe bananas will disintegrate when cooked. Peel the bananas and slice in half lengthwise then cut into chunks. In a mixing bowl, combine the bananas, ^{1}/$_2$ teaspoon of the salt and just enough cold water to cover the bananas. Set aside.
2 Bring the water to a boil in a pot or saucepan over medium heat. Add the dried sago pearls and cook, stirring occasionally, until the pearls are almost clear with tiny white spots in the center, about 7–10 minutes.
3 Drain the bananas and add to the sago pearls. Stir in the coconut cream, pandanus or vanilla extract and the remaining salt. Continue cooking until the bananas are tender, about 5–7 minutes.
4 Remove from the heat and serve warm.

Mango Lassis

1 1/2 cups (250 g) diced peeled ripe mango
1 1/2 cups (375 ml) yogurt
1/2 cup (125 ml) orange juice
2 tablespoons honey
1/2 teaspoon ground cardamom
Ice cubes

Serves 3
Preparation time: 10 mins

Combine all the ingredients in a blender and pulse until smooth and frothy. Pour into 3 tall glasses and serve immediately.

If preferred, you may replace the mango with ripe papaya to make **Papaya Lassi**. Combine 1 3/4 cups (300 g) ripe papaya cubes, 1 cup (250 ml) yogurt, 2 cups (500 ml) iced water, 2 tablespoons honey, 1 tablespoon lime juice, 1/2 teaspoon salt, 1/4 teaspoon black peppercorns, 1 tablespoon rose water and some ice cubes, and pulse in the blender in the same manner.

Sweet Potato in Sweet Ginger Syrup

2 medium orange or yellow sweet potatoes (about 12 oz/350g)
4 cups (1 liter) water
$1/2$ in (1 cm) fresh ginger, thinly sliced
1 pandanus leaf, tied into a knot
$1/3$–$1/2$ cup (65–100 g) fine granulated sugar (depending on sweetness desired)

1 Peel the sweet potatoes and cut into bite-sized chunks.
2 Rinse the sweet potato pieces, then place them in a medium-sized pan with the water, ginger and pandanus leaf. Bring to a boil, then reduce the heat to medium and cook until the sweet potato pieces are tender. Remove the ginger and pandanus leaf.
3 Sweeten to taste and serve warm or cold.

Serves 4–6
Preparation time: 15 mins
Cooking time: 20 mins

Red Rubies in Sweet Coconut Cream

12 water chestnuts
(about 12 oz/350 g),
peeled and finely diced
to yield 1 1/2 cups
1 teaspoon beetroot
juice (or a few drops of
red food coloring)
2 cups (500 ml) water
1/2 cup (60 g) cornstarch
Crushed ice, to serve
Mixed tropical fruits
(jackfruit, longans,
lychees, etc), diced to
yield 2 cups (optional)

Sweet Coconut Cream
1 cup (200 g) sugar
1/2 cup (125 ml) water
2 cups (500 ml) thick
coconut milk
1 teaspoon pandanus or
vanilla extract

Serves 6
Preparation time: 30 mins
Cooking time: 20 mins

1 To make the Sweet Coconut Cream, boil the sugar and water in a saucepan over medium heat for about 5 minutes, stirring constantly, until the sugar completely dissolves and a thick syrup is obtained. Remove from the heat and set aside to cool. Add the coconut milk and pandanus or vanilla extract, and mix well. Set aside.

2 Place the diced water chestnut in a bowl and sprinkle with the beetroot juice or red food coloring, creating light and dark red spots that resemble the look of rubies or pomegranate seeds. Soak the red diced water chestnut in 2 cups (500 ml) of water for at least 2 hours. Remove and drain.

3 Roll the red diced water chestnut in the cornstarch until coated on all sides, then place in a sieve and shake off any excess cornstarch. Set aside.

4 Bring a pot of water to a boil. In small batches, add the coated water chestnut into the pot, stirring gently to separate, and simmer for 2–3 minutes until they float to the surface. Remove with a slotted spoon or wire mesh and plunge into cold water for about 1 minute. Drain and set aside. Continue until all the water chestnut are cooked.

5 To serve, place some crushed ice in a dessert bowl and top with 3 tablespoons of the water chestnut rubies and 2 tablespoons of mixed tropical fruits (if using). Spoon 4 tablespoons of the Sweet Coconut Cream on top.

Frozen Bananas on a Stick

8 ripe finger bananas or 2 ripe regular bananas (approx 8 oz/250 g), cut into quarters
8 wooden ice cream sticks
1 cup (250 ml) coconut cream
2 tablespoons fine granulated sugar
$1/2$ teaspoon salt
1 cup (100 g) chopped roasted unsalted peanuts
4 tablespoons freshly grated coconut or dried coconut flakes

1 Peel the bananas and thread them onto the ice-cream sticks. Place on a plate, cover with plastic wrap and freeze in the freezer for $1–1^1/_2$ hours.

2 Combine the coconut cream, sugar and salt in a narrow glass and stir until the sugar completely dissolves.

3 On a plate, combine the peanuts and coconut, and mix well. Dip a frozen banana into the sweetened coconut cream, tilting the glass to ensure the banana is coated thoroughly. Remove and roll in the peanut mixture until the banana is coated on all sides, then place on a serving platter. Repeat with the remaining bananas.

4 Serve the coated bananas immediately, or return to the freezer until ready to serve.

Serves 4
Preparation time: 10 mins + 1$^1/_2$ hours freezing time

Refreshing Young Coconut Jelly Dessert

Bottom Layer
1 cup (250 ml) coconut juice (page 7)
1¹/₂ cups (375 ml) water
1 tablespoon gelatin powder
4 tablespoons sugar
¹/₄ teaspoon Pandanus Extract (page 8)

Top Layer
2 cups (500 ml) coconut juice (page 7)
¹/₂ cup (125 ml) thick coconut milk
¹/₂ tablespoon gelatin powder
1 tablespoon sugar
1 cup (250 g) young coconut flesh

1 Make the Bottom Layer first. Bring the coconut juice, water and gelatin to a boil in a saucepan over medium heat, stirring constantly. Add the sugar and Pandanus Extract and stir until the sugar completely dissolves. Remove from the heat and pour into a cake pan. Chill in the refrigerator until firm.
2 Make the Top Layer by bringing the coconut juice, water or coconut milk and gelatin to a boil in a saucepan over medium heat, stirring constantly. Add the sugar and stir until the sugar completely dissolves. Remove from the heat and stir in the coconut flesh. Pour the mixture over the Bottom Layer that has set in the cake pan. Chill in the refrigerator until the Top Layer is set, about 20 minutes.
3 Slice the coconut jelly into squares or diamond shapes and serve chilled.

Serves 4–6
Preparation time: 20 mins + 30 mins chilling
Cooking time: 10 mins

Vietnamese Iced Coffee

1$^1/_2$ cups (100 g) large black or white tapioca pearls

$^1/_2$ cup (30 g) gourmet dark roast coffee powder (French Roast, Espresso, etc.)

2$^1/_2$ cups (625 ml) water

2 tablespoons sugar

$^1/_3$ cup (80 ml) sweetened condensed milk

2 cups crushed ice

$^1/_2$ cup (125 ml) milk or cream

Serves 4–6
Preparation time: **20 mins**
Cooking time: **25 mins**

1 Cook the tapioca pearls in a pot of water until tender and fully expanded, about 10–15 minutes. Drain in a colander and place them in a bowl. Sprinkle with 1 tablespoon of sugar. Stir to mix well. Set aside.
2 Bring the water to a boil, add the ground coffee powder. Gently boil the coffee mixture for 7–10 minutes. Strain the mixture through a fine sieve or coffee filter and discard the solids. Alternatively, brew the ground coffee in a coffee maker (with filter) to get 2 cups of very rich, strong coffee.
3 Add the remaining sugar and condensed milk. Stir to mix well and set aside to chill in the refrigerator.
4 To serve, place about 2 tablespoons of the tapioca pearls at the bottom of each tall glass. Fill the glass with crushed ice. Pour the coffee mixture almost to the rim of the glass and top with milk or cream. Alternatively blend the coffee mixture, crushed ice and milk in a blender and pour on top of the tapioca pearls. Serve with large straws or small spoons.

Almond Jelly in Jackfruit Syrup

Crushed ice, to serve

Almond Jelly
1 tablespoon gelatin
  powder
$^1/_3$ cup (65 g) sugar
1 cup (250 ml) water
$1^1/_3$ cups (350 ml) milk
1 teaspoon almond extract

Jackfruit Syrup
1 cup (250 ml) water
1 cup (200 g) sugar
1 teaspoon vanilla extract
1 cup (200 g) sliced fresh
  or canned jackfruit

1 To make the Jackfruit Syrup, bring the water to a boil in a saucepan. Add the sugar and vanilla extract and simmer for 3–5 minutes, stirring constantly until the sugar completely dissolves and the mixture thickens to a thin syrup. Remove and set aside to cool. Add the sliced jackfruit and mix well.

2 To make the Almond Jelly, bring all the ingredients to a boil over medium heat in a saucepan, stirring constantly, then simmer for 5–7 minutes, until the gelatin completely dissolves. Remove from the heat and strain through a sieve into a small cake pan. Chill in the refrigerator until firm, about 30 minutes. Cut the Almond Jelly into little pieces.

3 To serve, fill individual serving bowls with the Almond Jelly, add the Jackfruit Syrup and top with crushed ice.

Serves 6
Preparation time: 20 mins + 30 mins chilling
Cooking time: 25 mins

Complete Recipe Listing